MIND AND HEART

MIND
AND
HEART

*Studies in Christian Truth
and Experience*

by

RONALD A. WARD
M.A., B.D., Ph.D.

London
MARSHALL, MORGAN & SCOTT
Edinburgh

LONDON
MARSHALL, MORGAN AND SCOTT, LTD.
1-5 PORTPOOL LANE
HOLBORN, E.C.1

AUSTRALIA AND NEW ZEALAND
117-119 BURWOOD ROAD
MELBOURNE E.13

SOUTH AFRICA
P.O. BOX 1720, STURK'S BUILDINGS
CAPE TOWN

U.S.A.
BAKER BOOK HOUSE
GRAND RAPIDS
MICHIGAN

*Printed in Great Britain by C. Tinling & Co. Ltd.,
Liverpool, London and Prescot*

PREFACE

THE AIM OF this book is to give an outline of the main Christian doctrines with a certain lightness of touch and with the warmth of Christian experience. In the hope that it may be of service to ministers and Christian workers generally the illustrations have been retained. Though the chapters are not in sermonic form, they represent the substance of my preaching and teaching over the last decade. The material has been used in sermons in church services and in lectures at clergy conferences, rural deaneries, youth groups and other societies. Some of it was given in addresses to the students at Tyndale Hall, Bristol, and some to the Islington Clerical Conference. I drew on it for lectures at the Ministers Conference on Evangelism held in Dalhousie University at the close of the Leighton Ford Crusade in the city of Halifax, Nova Scotia. A Convocation is an occasion for a wider utterance than an address directed at the graduating class and one chapter was given as a Graduation Address to the Anglican Women's Training College in the city of Toronto. Part of the contents has been in print before in *The Evangelical Christian*, *The Church of England Newspaper* and *The Canadian Churchman*, though it has been revised and some additions have been made. I should like to acknowledge the kindness of the Editors and of the friends, known and unknown, who have listened—or read—with sympathy and encouragement.

During thirty years in the ministry a man acquires a store of material in his mind, the source of which he often cannot trace. Memory plays its tricks and if I have offended I apologize.

Once more I gratefully acknowledge help from my wife.

R.A.W.

TO
PHILIP
in the hope that he will become
another apostle

CONTENTS

THE BIBLE—THE WRITTEN WORD

IT IS SIGNIFICANT that God has chosen *words* to be the focus of His self-disclosure. He did not, for example, choose music or painting. It is true that we may feel inspired by noble music. We may be so uplifted that we go forth to wage the Christian fight with greater devotion. But either the music (as with a hymn) brings with it a reminder of its words, or a genuinely "wordless" music stirs us to remembrance of Christian truth; or else, if it stir us at all, our emotion is purely secular. It may be deep. The big drum of a military band, we are told, makes men want to fight. But the cause for which they fight is an open matter.

This view may be contested. Some people say that great music to them is as good as a sermon. They should be carefully questioned. What did the music *tell* them? Can they pass on the message to others? Will it put them right with God? As a matter of fact music has been described as the means by which emotion is transferred from one person to another. Its intellectual content is vague. It is not for nothing that the early preachers told the story of the cross and laid bare its meaning. They did not go into a new city and whistle or hum! This is the Christian counterpart to the Platonic subordination of the music to the words.

We can speak in much the same way about painting. It is possible for a Christian to be moved to a deeper allegiance when he sees a picture of the crucifixion, or to feel the challenge of Holman Hunt's *Light of the World*. But that is surely because he knows so much already. The pictures may arouse curiosity in one who has never met the Christian faith. It can hardly tell him that Christ died for his sins. All art, including music and painting, is "ministerial." It may be used in the service of the faith. John Bunyan knew this when he spoke of "Eyegate" and many present-day Christian educators are following his lead. A servant, however, (which is what "ministerial" means) has to work with other servants, and to be under a master. Ultimately the words are supreme. The picture needs to be explained; the music has to be supplemented. The final appeal is to language.

In ritual and ceremonial we see living art in motion. Deeds are louder than words, it is said, and we know what is meant. But there can be hypocritical handshakes and even the apparent act of kindness may have ulterior motives. Ritual may create a mood in the observers but it is the words which convey the message. Even a silent ritual would be a mime or dumb show unless it had a meaning, and the meaning must be expressed in words. We may feel a sense of gratitude to God for His mercy, but how did we know that He is merciful? There is a place for silent worship and its spell may be strong. Even so we return words to God as the expression of the thankfulness and praise of our hearts. "O Lord, open Thou my lips; and my mouth shall tell the story of Thy praise."

What, then, shall we say of that sum total of words which go to make up Holy Scripture? How shall we describe the Bible? At the outset we should notice just exactly what it is.

It is correct to state that when God disclosed Himself to men He did so in mighty acts. "He made known His ways unto Moses, His acts unto the children of Israel." The acts of God are to be seen in both history and nature. The Old Testament *kerygma*[1] tells how "the Lord brought us forth out of Egypt . . . and He hath brought us into this place, and hath given us this land. . . ." And in addition "the heavens declare the glory of God." Israel was taken across the Red Sea and thus escaped the clutches of Pharaoh. Would the people have known that it was God who delivered them, if Moses had not told them? Would they have known that the heavens declare the glory, not of nature, but of God, if a prophetic voice had not told them that "by the word of the Lord were the heavens made"? To that extent the unit of revelation is the interpreted event. But interpretation requires language.

Was it interpretation when it was affirmed that "the Lord our God is one Lord"? When it was claimed that the Lord is God; that there is none else beside Him; that the gods of the heathen are idols; and that worship is to be directed to the Lord alone: was that the interpretation of an "event"? It might perhaps be argued that the event in question is the whole world and universe in time and space and that creation is ascribed to the one God. But this is not the work of God in history like the Exodus. The bare statement of the unity and uniqueness of God is more than

[1] "Proclamation"

an interpretation. "The Lord our God is one Lord" is a statement of truth which stands in its own right.

That is to say, it is more than a mere inference. It was the Greeks
in the ancient world who sought wisdom and loved the philosophic tracing of clues and the development of thought. But God
is not the conclusion of an argument. He was a Presence made
known to His prophets. "As the Lord liveth, before Whom I
stand." How they were aware of Him is their secret, though
those who have met Him in Christ in personal, experiential faith
may have a sound clue.

Thought is not ruled out, of course, from biblical religion.
The Bible would be the poorer if we were to take away all the
passages containing the words "therefore" or "because." It may
be that we know some truths about God by inference. After all,
the apostle Paul inferred from the fact of justification by faith
that we should go on to enjoy peace with God. But believing
men not only know truths about God. They know Him.

In some measure God has disclosed Himself to all men, as we
learn from the first chapter of the Epistle to the Romans. Men
suppress the truth indeed in their life of unrighteousness, but the
truth is there. He has manifested His invisible attributes to men;
that is, He has made available to their awareness His eternal
power and deity. There is enough in the universe around us for
men to discern such attributes; enough to make them responsible
before God.

And more than responsible: they have no legitimate defence.
With such knowledge of God—or in spite of it—they do not
glorify Him. They do not recognize His being, His character, His
majesty and His might. They withhold from Him their thanksgiving. Their reasoning is unproductive; their knowledge is but
a groping in darkness; mind and conscience are alike unintelligent. They claim wisdom; in fact they are foolish. The result is
idolatry.

All this was true in the day when Paul wrote. It is true today
and the weight of responsibility is greater. Astronomy has pushed
the frontiers of the universe almost to infinity; atomic research
has discovered the infinitesimal. The "expanding" universe is
great; but God is greater. He is the Creator and Sustainer. If His
attributes are discerned because they are to be grasped from what
He has made, then they should be known even more surely from
men's increasing knowledge.

This revelation of God is all around us. His power and deity
may be known by the use of the telescope, the microscope and

even the naked eye. It is enough to make all men guilty. But it contains no gospel in which men can hope. The revelation is not complete.

God chose a people to whom He revealed Himself in a special way. It could be argued that revelation came to the Greeks also. Not all the discoveries of the philosophers were wrong. But Israel alone was the elect nation: "you only have I known of all the families of the earth." To Israel alone was it given to know God as one and as righteous. The laws and ceremonies, types and sacrifices, nurture a people in the truth that the approach to God is not to be taken for granted. It is a fearful thing to fall into the hands of the living God and it is a solemn experience even to approach Him. Nobody must presume. To Israel alone was given the sure promise of a coming Saviour. Thus the Old Testament by itself is incomplete. It is a book of hope. Just as some journalists write "more" at the bottom of every page of typescript, so that the typesetter may not finish prematurely; so every page of the Old Testament, including the last, should have "more" at the foot of the page. It is the dictionary to the New Testament indeed. We should not understand that "Christ our Passover is sacrificed for us" without the Old Testament. But until He came, the Saviour of the world, the Old Testament awaits its climax.

And then He came. He did not only speak the Word of God. He was, and is, the Word of God. "In the beginning was the Word, and the Word was with God and the Word was God. . . . And the Word was made flesh. . . ." When God spoke His creative Word "in the beginning," the Son of God, the eternal Word, was there. In Him resides all the fullness of the Godhead. All revelation is summed up in Him. All that had been given in nature to manifest the eternal power and deity of God; all that the prophets had said and the Old Testament had taught; all is taken up into Him—and transcended. He did not merely repeat the message of the prophets. He *is* the message.

Christ is the complete, not the incomplete, revelation of God. We have heard much recently of the appropriate "images" of God. Christ is the true Image of God; He is "the image of the invisible God" for, as He said, "he that hath seen Me hath seen the Father." Creation is a partial revelation. It tells of God's power and deity and makes men to be without excuse. It does not tell of God's intentions; it has no gospel. The Old Testament points to One Who would come but its writers could only look forward. In their day He had not come, and they could not look back and see Him on the firm rock of history. Now the promised

One has come, Himself the very Word of God. All that God would have men know of Himself is contained in Christ. There is nothing further to come which would conflict with what we already have in Him; nothing further which would enrich His personality. All of deity is packed into Christ.

We should observe that the complete revelation of God is in the complete Christ. It is to be found not only in what He said; not only in what He was and is; not only in what He did; but in all three together. There are those who would see the whole of the Christian faith in the Sermon on the Mount; but this makes the cross an unnecessary luxury. Others see in the Man Himself all that we need to know. But this does not show us how His Person can benefit ours. Yet others see in His deeds of kindness a sign of what God is like, forgetting our Lord's stern words to express the divine reaction against sin. The full unveiling of God in Christ is in His Person, His words and His work.

In His Person we see One Who had an intimate knowledge of God. It is possible for a man to be skilled in theology and a master of doctrine; but to have no acquaintance with God. Christ knew God. Except for that bitter hour of dereliction on the cross, which has its own explanation, He was always in fellowship with His Father. If ever a man on earth knew where he was to find the living God, Christ had that secret. He constantly walked with God. If any man could tell us about God, He could. And His communion with His Father was never marred by sin.

His life was the perfect life of utter sinlessness. He did no deed for which He should seek repentance; no unworthy thought entered His mind, no false ambition, nothing unclean, nothing unloving, which had to be ejected with sorrow and shame. He knew God, and as Man He lived in the utter perfection of God.

But He did not live thus in silence. From His deep inner knowledge of God He spoke to men. He told them of the Father's character: of His goodness and His love. His message was not one-sided: He spoke also of God's opposition to sin, not as a mere abstraction but as embodied in sinful men. He described some sinful men as an abomination in the sight of God. It would seem from this that God is both for men and against men. The holy God is opposed to sinners and at the same time loves them. (It has been said that God is no man's Enemy. That is correct. He is still, however, the Opponent of sinners.) This double attitude of God would be an insoluble puzzle if it were not for the Old Testament "dictionary" to explain, and the actual work of Christ on the cross. There He died for sinful men, bearing the weight of

God's judgment on sin. The "opposition" of God to sin came
into its focus on the cross. At the same time the cross sets forth
the love of God for sinners. Justice and mercy have kissed each
other; holiness and love are at one. The one God, righteous and
holy, the Creator beside Whom there is no other, has revealed
Himself completely and finally in Jesus. All earlier revelation
converges on the cross; all evangelism and all the growth of the
people of God radiates from it. It is the final answer to sin and the
supreme light on destiny. Paul sums it all up in the succinct
phrase, "the word of the cross."

Now the Lord Christ dwelt in Palestine, a little country at the
world's crossroads. It is true that "this thing was not done in a
corner." It was done in Jerusalem; in Palestine; in the inhabited
world: not in the secret recesses of a far-off heaven. Even so, how
are men to receive the divine disclosure in Christ? They do not
know it automatically. In some way they have to be told.

It would seem that there must be one of three possibilities. If
all men in all the world and through all the centuries are to
receive God's good news in Christ, either there must be a continuing revelation or an immortal apostolate or an authentic
record.

There is a sense, as we shall see, in which revelation is continued. Every time the gospel is preached in the power of the
Holy Spirit there is a revelation of God. Every time Scripture is
read under the illumination of the same Spirit God is made known
to men. Every time an authentic believer prays scripturally there
is a listening ear of the Most High. And at the Second Advent
there will be further revelation, when every eye shall see Him.

But this is not a revelation, added to what has already been
given in Christ. The Holy Spirit testifies to the Word and is
never separate from the Word. He owns the preached Word as
His; He owns the written Word as His; it is through Him that the
living and ascended Christ is known in experience. In the Spirit
Christ is present; in Christ God is present. And at the Second
Advent it will be the same Christ returning to gather up His own.
And if an unbeliever reads or hears Holy Scripture without the
awakening of faith within him, God is sufficiently revealed in His
demands upon men for them to be responsible beings and
accountable to Him.

In that sense revelation is continued. But that is quite different
from a mere repetition. All this "continuation" is an unfolding of
what is already present in Christ. The once-for-all revelation in
Christ is not repeated. That would mean that Bethlehem and

Calvary would have to take place in every generation. Could the ascended Christ become once again a Baby in Bethlehem? How could He? He is already human as well as divine. He has taken the Manhood into God and remains for ever, God and Man. There is something distastefully artificial about the thought of His becoming a Baby again.

Could He appear on earth again as a Man? He could, no doubt. But it would lead up once more to Golgotha. If He died a second time on the cross, a third time, a fourth time, as many times as there are to be generations on the earth; then either His first death on the cross was inadequate; or if it were adequate every later experience of death would be no more than a sombre pageant, an artificial enactment from which the power had been withdrawn. It would be an exhibition, and no more than an exhibition, of the externals of a former inner experience. God has not chosen that method.

The Lord when on earth chose men as His apostles. They were to witness to His continuing ministry from the time of the baptism of John up to the ascension. They were to testify to the same Jesus: from His baptism, through His public ministry to His death, His resurrection and His exaltation to the right hand of the Father. They were His witnesses. But the world could not be told the good news in their generation. Even if it were, who would tell their sons, their grandsons and all their descendants?

Could the apostles be endowed with immortality on earth? No doubt they could, if God so willed it. But in every generation they would have been the most hard-worked group of men on earth! The number of questions which would have to be referred to them for decision in the light of their knowledge of Christ would take all their time and halt the work of evangelism. In any case there is an element of the grotesque in the thought of men growing older and older and never dying. They would have to have "resurrection-bodies" before their own resurrection. Whatever the difficulties and however easily omnipotence could have overcome them, God has not chosen that method.

God in His wisdom has chosen to give us an authentic apostolic record of the fact and details of Christ, a record which enshrines the apostolic witness and is thus the successor to the apostles. Bethlehem and Calvary are not repeated. Christ being raised from the dead dies no more. The apostles have gone home to Him. But they have left behind a record of revelation, a revelation which is incarnate in Christ, interpreted by the apostles through the Holy Spirit, as our Lord promised, and preserved in Holy Scripture.

This carries with it the Old Testament as well as the New. For the apostolic record leaves us in no doubt about our Lord's attitude to the Hebrew scriptures. For Him, Who is the complete revelation of God, the Old Testament is the Word of God. Thus Old and New Testaments together constitute a record of revelation.

It is not a "bare" record. Scripture itself partakes of the nature of revelation. It is not only a historical account of what happened in the past. It is the medium through which God has chosen to make known His Son. To this very day men preach the Word of God—and their message is the Word written; to this very day the Holy Spirit speaks to men's heart—when the Word written is preached or read.

The Bible must not be so treated that we are left with it in our hands—and on our hands. To be left with it on our hands would mean that we are embarrassed by it, uncertain what we should do with it. But it is the apostolic witness made permanent. It contains indeed a selection. John tells us that there are many other deeds which Jesus did and are unrecorded. We have thus an apostolic selection. The ethical interest of the apostles—to say nothing of the Holy Spirit—ensures that the right selection has been made.

What, then, is the Bible? It is the Word of God written. It testifies to Christ, the living Word. Yet there are not two Words but one Word. The living Word is made known through the written Word. The written Word testifies to the living Word.

There is a parallel between the living Word and the written Word. Just as the complete revelation of God is given in the complete Christ, so the apostolic testimony to the complete Christ is found in the complete Scripture. There is no possible test which will enable us or allow us to pick and choose and say that this text is the Word of God and that text is not. Different texts may make their different appeals to different men at different times. It is obvious that "God is love" has more appeal than "David begat Solomon," both intellectually and emotionally; though even here, if Spurgeon was right, we can start with the "unpromising" text, break through a hedge and race across country "to Jesus." We are grateful to the words of Dr. J. W. C. Wand, lately Bishop of London. He tells us, in the evening of a long and learned life, that the title, Word of God, applies to the whole Bible and not to mere parts of it.

We have, then, the Word of God written. It follows that we should observe what it purposes. It has not been given to us by the Bible Societies; by the Sunday Schools; by the church at large; and ultimately by the living God Himself; merely to be kept in a domestic museum as an interesting relic of the past. It has a purpose.

Its function is to be a mirror. We might have used the word "portrait," only we all know the man who dislikes the pictures of himself. They are distorted, out of focus and fail to do him justice! The mirror, however, reflects him just as he is. When we honestly read the Bible we see not only the portrait of the other man; we look into a mirror and see ourselves. And men do not like what they see. Through the ministry of the Holy Spirit they recognize themselves. The Bible shows men precisely what they are. It reveals to them their inner thoughts, their private ambitions, their jealousies and envies, their spiritual vulgarity, their false conclusions and their temper of rebellion. It shows man strutting on the stage of his life, a would-be king with a bankrupt treasury.

The Bible purposes to be an alarm-bell. Solemnly it sounds its warning note. There are quicksands and rocks ahead, and if men do not change their course their leaky ship will crash to final ruin and wreck. Yet men are blind to their danger and do not wish to heed. But still the bell tolls. Men pride themselves on being the captain of their own ship but they have not gained their Master's Ticket. They are not even good members of the crew. They cannot live together. Wars and rivalries, military and political, economic and social, divide them from one another. Police in vast numbers are required to deter the crime and to catch the criminal. Accounts are subject to inspection to counteract fraud. A multiplicity of acts of Parliament or Congress grows with the years, to control our complicated life, and sanctions and penalties are attached to enforce obedience. Spies are everywhere, partly because men do not trust one another and partly because of national ambition. The trouble is deep within ourselves, for we are a fallen race. And still the Bible sounds to call us from our folly.

It is a medicine for our malady. Man, left to his own devices, could not have discovered it. Still less could he have invented it. There is but one remedy for the ills to which men fall heir, one remedy alone. There is no other Name under heaven given among men whereby we must be saved. It is a given Name, not a Name bought or inherited or forced out of an unwilling heaven; a Name undeserved. It is an exclusive Name, for there is no other. That is the true intolerance of the Christian faith; an intolerance which should be courteous in all social life and uncompromising in witness. It is a compulsory Name: we must be saved by that Name. Salvation is God's command.

And so the Bible purposes to give an invitation. It is earnest in its approach, for it knows what is at stake and knows the cost of man's deliverance. But men persist in not taking it seriously. "They made light of it." It is a sign of the moral and spiritual seriousness of the Bible that in the providence of God it has continued so long and still invites men to the gospel. It protests at the opposition and the indifference of men but they fail to see the love behind the protest.

It has large promises. Blessed is the man indeed who puts his trust in the Lord. He is promised the removal of guilt, the possession of power, an exhilaration in life and the abiding presence in his heart of the living Christ. Large promises! But men belittle them, to their hurt; not knowing what they do but responsible for their culpable ignorance. The pattern for living is but the promise in the imperative mood. God has so constituted the world that it will only work one way, His way. The "moral duties" of the Christian life set forth in Scripture are not meant to be taken as a secular and loveless grinding out of "good deeds" but the glad following of disciples for whom their Lord has done everything.

In particular a destiny is unveiled to give men a long look at the life they live. There is a fork in the road, and the resulting two roads lead to their respective ends. The one is dark and forbidding, a horror which man could not have created—and he has created some terrifying things in his time. The other is bright with the light of God's eternal Son for the eternal delectation of men who believe in Him. There have been noble creations made by man the artist, but nothing to compare with this. It is the consummation of the gospel which the Bible enshrines and proclaims.

The purpose of the Bible is thus solemnly to show men what they are; earnestly to tell them what God in Christ has done for them; affectionately to call them through the Spirit to turn to Christ; and spaciously to promise them vast blessings. It seeks to create experience and to test experience. It would renew their hearts and keep them renewed. It is a fount to inspire and an authority to correct. If it is rejected it still has authority. And to speak in very human language, it will be produced as evidence on the Day of Judgment.

Finally we should not fail to observe how the Bible "works." The spoken words of Jesus have been described as "truth with impact." The "impact" is still made when the Word is read.

Organizations like the Scripture Gift Mission and the Bible Societies are constantly finding examples of this, as their reports show. A striking example, however, comes from the nineteenth century. I remember as a boy being told by my father of William Haslam, the high church clergyman who was converted through one of his own sermons! Dr. J. Edwin Orr has told the story again, rescuing the details from Haslam's aged son in Australia. The text was: "Therefore being justified by faith we have peace with God through our Lord Jesus Christ." Haslam was in the pulpit, and he paused in his address as he realized the truth of the text. A discerning—and somewhat eccentric—evangelist was in the congregation and seeing what had happened he shouted out: "Hallelujah! the parson's converted!" Haslam became a powerful evangelist.

Holy Scripture, then, "works" as it is read. It is the same when it is preached. But in its preaching it must be wielded as a sword, to thrust and cut and pierce. It is not a culprit in the dock. It needs no defence, still less an apology. The early preachers were sublimely confident, though their confidence did not rest in themselves. "The Word of the Lord abideth for ever. And this is the Word which was preached to you." How many of us, preachers as we are, so saturate our sermons with the Word of God that we can declare to men that "thus saith the Lord"—and that this Word which we now preach endures for ever?

The Word of God written is self-authenticating. When God discloses Himself He needs no references to support Him, no testimonial of character. The Holy Spirit interprets the Word preached or read and it comes to men's hearts as *God's* Word. It may be freely admitted that it has its human aspects. It is written in human language, in human style and figure. We find Mark rather than Luke the physician recording that the Woman with the Issue had received much medical treatment—and got worse! Here we may compare the Bible with our Lord Himself, as Dr. G. W. Bromiley has shown us. He, too, is both divine and human. And, like Him, the Bible "knows what is in man." It is powerful, it "works," because the Holy Spirit inspired it and owns it and uses it. So, too, our Lord went "in the power of the Spirit." The Holy Spirit is never separate from the Word. He does not initiate revelation: that is a Montanist aberration; He illumines a revelation already given. "He shall glorify Me."

Can the Bible ever become a dead letter? Yes, it can. If our knowledge is merely academic or speculative; if we have no personal interest in the writings and no desire for the blessings;

if we are unprayerful and unbelieving; then for us it is no more than the printed page. "A veil rests on our reading; a veil rests on our heart. But when we turn to the Lord the veil is removed." When the God Who said "Let there be light" thus creatively shines in our hearts, then the "dead letter" or mere print becomes for us, as it is in itself, the lively Word. As "dead letter" it is still evidence to condemn our unbelief; as lively Word, through the ministry of the Holy Spirit, it can mean life from the dead.

Therefore we should seek not only information but also illumination; not only good notions but in Christ a new nature.

2

THE WORD MADE FLESH

WE CAN AT times illustrate Christian truth by commonplace occurrences. For example there was the day when the housewife put the meat into the oven to cook while she went out to buy groceries at the store. She had timed everything so carefully. She would catch the bus; call at the Post Office and mail some letters; cross the road to the grocer's, purchase everything on her list and then take the bus home. On arrival she would cook a few vegetables and prepare the dinner table. By that time the meat would be done to a turn.

But something went wrong. There were so many people in the grocer's that twice the normal time was needed. Then on coming out she met the minister, who kept her talking for ten minutes. Then she "bumped into" a friend whom she had not seen for months. More time was consumed and the bus was lost. When she did finally reach home the meat was burnt.

That was before the day of the automatic oven, which shuts off the heat at the right moment! The housewife was annoyed, of course, and tempted to exclaim angrily. "Bother the oven! It's always going wrong!" But has it gone wrong? What has really happened? The oven has been behaving perfectly. It has been doing exactly what it was set to do: to go on heating until somebody or something stops it. In other words, it has just been obeying the laws of its being.

We find the same sort of thing happening elsewhere. We come and find that the battery of our automobile is dead. By mistake we had left the engine turned on; or had forgotten to switch off the parking lights. The battery has gone on working—as it was meant to by its maker.

Again: in a small town a generation ago a wedding was celebrated between a somewhat elderly couple, and to avoid publicity it was held early in the morning. After the service in church the bridal couple entered the car to be driven to the hotel for the wedding breakfast. They ought to have been happy. In actual fact they were very distressed if not angry. The motor horn stuck and they were driven through the town with its raucous noise drawing attention to them: The very thing they had wanted to avoid had happened. No doubt the driver was blamed for his inability and the horn or hooter for its behaviour. But it was not to be blamed. Like the cooker and the battery, it had merely been obeying the law of its being. It was meant to sound—until turned off.

We have spoken of a "law." Where did it come from? It came from the mind of the inventor. He used his mind in making the design of the cooker, the battery or the motor horn, whichever we are thinking about, and they bear traces of his mind. What started as an idea in his mind became a design, and the design became embodied in a thing—cooker, battery or motor horn. As Plato might have said, the inventor was intelligent and his inventions were intelligible. They went on working because nobody had turned them off. That is how they were made. They follow certain laws, mechanical indeed, but still laws, the rules by which they work. They are principles and are reason-able, because they come from reason (i.e. the mind of their inventor), and might be called a "plan."

This is not limited to cookers and cars but is found in all the world. Thus, because of its reason or plan, an acorn becomes an oak. It cannot grow into anything else. It will never become a pine or a railway engine. An avalanche flows down the mountainside and does not take off like an aircraft just because a village stands in its way. Water freezes in cold weather, without stopping to wonder if it will make all the traffic pile up in confusion or burst its pipes and cause flooding.

Each works according to its own inner law, principle or plan. This happens in all the world. And the world as a whole does the same. It has its own principle or plan, no doubt very complicated and no doubt containing within itself all the plans of all the objects which make up the world. But it has its own plan.

This is because it has its own Planner. The design of the Maker is seen in the finished product. The world is intelligible because its Maker is intelligent; reason-able because its Maker is Reason— just as the cooker or automobile is intelligible because its inventor is intelligent.

Now the Greek thinkers used to call this principle, this law or reason in accordance with which things work, their *logos*, which is sometimes translated "reason," sometimes "account" and some- times "word." When they stated how a thing works or when they defined it, they were fond of speaking of "giving an account of it." And the world as a whole has an account, a "theory" or a *logos*, which is derived from its Maker. But who did make the world?

In the beginning God created the heaven and the earth. Thus the plan, the principle, the account, the theory or reason which we see in all things and in the world as a whole is derived from God. If the world is reason-able, then so is its Author. God is Reason. But this is not the end of the story. Scripture teaches us that our Lord Jesus Christ was God's Agent in creation. Thus the plan or reason found in the world is derived from the reason which is the Mind of Christ.

Further, Christ is the Image of the invisible God. He is the radiance of His glory and the very stamp of His nature.

Two consequences follow. The reason in the world ("its intelligibility") is the outer expression of the inner reason in Christ; and Christ Himself is the outer expression of the inner reason in God. God spoke—and what He said was Christ. Hence we can say that in the beginning was reason and reason was with God and reason was God . . . all things came into being through reason. This is an unfamiliar translation and its flavour is somewhat Greek and intellectual; but it is still true. Even so there is yet more to be said, giving a further side to the picture.

I believe that it was the late Dr. F. W. Boreham who pointed out with astonishment that when God decided to create the world the instrument He chose to use was—speech. God spake—and it was done. God *said*, "Let there be light"; and there was light. "By the *word* of the Lord were the heavens made." That Word was and is Christ.

Now God has done many things beside making the world and expressing reason therein. How often do we read that "the Word of the Lord came unto. . . ." how often do we read the prophetic utterance, "Thus saith the Lord." The Word of God came in New Testament times also and men went everywhere, preaching the Word. The Word of God is saving. It is moral and spiritual as well as intellectual. It expresses the purpose of salvation as well as theoretical reason.

Thus we have two parallel lines. There is reason in the world which is the outer expression of the inner reason of Christ; and Christ Himself Who is the outer expression of the inner reason of God. And parallel to this one line of reason is the line of salvation. In the world, corresponding to the reason just mentioned, is the written Word and the Word preached, that is the gospel. It is the outer expression of the inner saving purpose in Christ; and Christ

Himself is the outer expression of the inner saving purpose in God. Thus in a further sense God spoke—and what He said was Christ.

In all this the key is Christ. He is God's reason and God's salvation. And Christ Himself set His reason in the universe and His preachers in the world. He is the Reason of God and of the world. He is the Salvation of God and the Light and Life of men. He is one with God and in Him both reason and salvation are united. Christ is Reason but He is not mere reason. He is God's *Logos*, the metaphysical and soteriological Word, God's principle of reason and His power of salvation.

Christ is thus Master in two realms: He is Ruler of Nature and Head of the Church. As God's Agent He created the universe and gave it intelligibility; and He redeemed sinful men. That is why a German hymn of the seventeenth century can say:

> Fairest Lord Jesus,
>   Ruler of all nature
>
> None can be nearer, fairer or dearer,
> Than Thou, my Saviour, art to me.

Nature is not left alone. The Ruler is also the Saviour.

This unity of the reason-able Word with the saving Word implies the unity of creation and salvation. It does not mean that the man who has been created is thereby automatically saved. It does mean that the Creator and the Redeemer are one. This should be the cause of deep thankfulness in Christian men. For consider the alternative.

Suppose that the Creator were not the Redeemer or the Redeemer not the Creator. Moral philosophers tell us that the moral life makes demands on the universe. They mean that the world which is the setting of our lives is not so alien to us that morality is impossible. It is not implied by this that goodness is possible or impossible. "Morality" here means the behaviour which is subject to the moral judgment, whether of approval or disapproval. If, then, the moral life of personalities requires a setting which does not prevent a life of conduct, good or bad morally, how much more does the activity of a Saviour require a "sympathetic" universe!

For consider: suppose our Lord had purposed the salvation of men but the universe was alien. Suppose He sought to save men but found the universe, the setting of His attempted work, hostile and able to prevent it. It would not tolerate His life and death and resurrection; it would make impossible the offering of prayer and our Lord's answers to prayer; it would hold up all the activity of His grace. But He is Master of the universe. It cannot thwart His plan. Creation flowed from His hand and remains in His control. He is unencumbered. He is free to save.

On the other hand, suppose Him to be Master of the universe but uninterested in men's salvation. Then were we lost indeed! In the mercy of God the divine Word is Lord of all.

And the Word was made flesh. This is the message which is prominent—or should be—at Christmas. No doubt Santa Claus has a place in our tradition, and it could be quite innocuous. But he has no place in the Christian pulpit. It could be argued that the Christian faith is ultimately responsible for the fact that unwanted babies are no longer exposed at birth, abandoned to cold and death. And it is understandable that babyhood should be in our minds at Christmas. But the Christmas season must not be allowed to be no more than the cult of the baby. A sound theology can be wrecked on the perfect baby. It would be boorish and surly to resent the many happy re-unions at Christmas time and we have no wish to do so. But Christmas is more than the festival of the family. The Word was made flesh.

God spoke—and His reason-able Word was Christ. God spoke—and His saving Word was Christ. The divine *Logos*, God's intellectual Reason and His saving purpose, became Man without ceasing to be God, and thereby took the first step on earth for our salvation. The unseen God, hitherto with clouds and darkness about His throne, has begun to be manifested. "That which was from the beginning, which we have heard, which we have seen with our eyes, which we gazed upon and our hands felt, concerning the Word of life . . . we are proclaiming to you also, that you also may have fellowship with us." As these men preached the living Word they retained the original impact in their memories: His voice was ever ringing in their ears and His human form constantly rose up in their imagination. The place of such vivid memories is today taken by the living Holy Spirit within us, sent by the same living Word.

That unknown God has been made known through His Son. That is why Charles Wesley could sing exultantly:

> Veiled in flesh the Godhead see;
> Hail the incarnate Deity!
> Pleased as Man with man to dwell,
> Jesus, our Immanuel.

Or even more simply:

> Our God contracted to a span,
> Incomprehensively made Man.

From all this certain inferences may be drawn. To begin with as Christians we know our earthly home. It is Christ's world. We do not stop short with a philosophical statement. It is true that this is reason's world; but it does not go far enough. Reason has walked the earth and has been seen to be warm with feeling. Bare reason might be coldly known in the abstract; in Christ we meet Reason as a Friend. In this world which came from Him, nothing is lost sight of; nothing is out of control. If appearances seem dark, it is still His house. Earthquakes may shatter towns; volcanoes may erupt and lightning strike. The scientific reason may be clear but the moral and spiritual purpose puzzling. The darkness may seem deep but it is His world. There are dark corners in many houses, but the owners own them all. And here the Owner is Christ, Who though He was rich for our sakes became poor that we through His poverty might be made rich. If we see a lurking danger, then for us:

> not a single shaft can hit
> till the love of God sees fit.

If this is Christ's world, for He made it, we might remind the student of science that he owes his very studies to Christ. After his graduation he may begin his work of scientific research in university or in industry. He should be told that he owes his very livelihood to Christ. Without Christ there would be no natural law to be studied and no scientific data to afford him a living. The student or the practitioner in any branch of science is as much in debt to Christ as the most devoted disciple. This world is Christ's house and we thus know our earthly home.

Again, if we are believers in Him, we know that we are alive. In the Word was life. Indeed He came that men might have life, and have it more abundantly. The authentic Christian, instructed in the faith, is assured of the life within himself because he is sure of the One Who gave him life. He trusts the word of Him Who promised and he knows from his own experience what it is to be dead and what it is to be alive in Christ. And he knows from the like experience of others with whom he is in fellowship. We know that we have passed from death to life because we love the brethren. This is more than an ethical test. It is a deep satisfaction in the companionship of likeminded friends, who, like us, have met with Christ and found life in Him. "He who believes in Me, even if he die, will live, and everyone who lives and believes in Me will never die."

All believing men need to be reminded of this from time to time. But it is essentially a reminder. It is not the giving of unsuspected information. A newly married man, for example, may be told immediately after the ceremony that a lawyer is waiting to hand him the deeds of a house—a wedding present which he had not anticipated or even thought about. It is possible to be married and not receive such a gift! But it is hardly possible to believe in Christ in the New Testament sense without, in the very fact of believing, the experience of a quickening of spirit. "I am writing this to you that you may know that you have eternal life, yes, you who believe in the Name of the Son of God."

Once more, we know where we are. In the Word was life, and the life was the light of men. We may think of the light as the sun, lighting up the whole countryside. Or we may think of it as a flashlight which shines about our feet. We may not see the distant scene. One step may be enough for us; one step at a time, with the light playing on our feet at every step. The Light keeps on shining in the darkness and the darkness has not overwhelmed it. The Christian may not see the road half a mile ahead. We live by faith and not by sight. But through the Word Who is his light he can see the ground at his feet. When he steps forward the light follows, so that he is always within a circle of light. If he steps into the darkness—keep within the circle of light! In this sense the Christian need never lose his way. He may not know where he is in relation to the nearest city, so to speak. It is enough to know that he is in the light. In that position he is not lost.

We do not sufficiently reflect that Christ is the Reason of God. He gives eternal life to His people and they will never perish; and no one will snatch them out of His hand. Even in the small circle of light we may dread the surrounding darkness. But if we remember that we are in His hand—and His grip is firm—our fear should pass. For in Him love is combined with reason, and He Who is creative Reason can penetrate the darkness. He knows the whole scene and knows the route.

Finally, we know that we are God's children. The Word made flesh did not give us arguments for the existence of God. He shared His sonship with us. His is indeed by nature; ours is by grace. But it is no less sonship. To those who received Him He gave the right to become children of God, because He Himself is the Lamb of God Who takes away the sin of the world. The barriers are down and God receives us as His sons.

Not all men are aware of such a sonship. It is either because they have never heard of it or, if they have heard of it, they have rejected it. Even His own received Him not. We should bless His Name that we are in His family or we should put ourselves there by receiving the living Word.

Thus we need never worry, for this world is Christ's house. We shall never perish, for as believers we have eternal life in Him. We need never lose our way, for we have light in Him and are in His hand. And we never need doubt, for we have sonship in Christ. And it is all because the Word was made flesh.

At the season of Christmas we naturally remember—or should remember—that Mary held in her arms the Child Who was the Creator of the world; that Reason had come within the range of unreasonable men; and that grace and truth, though of heavenly origin, had embarked on an earthly career, to encounter those who desired neither grace nor truth. All this should be in our minds. But we must not stop at Bethlehem. The world was not redeemed by the incarnation. We must not forget that, even as we celebrate Christmas, the Child must not be eternally left in babyhood. He advanced in wisdom and stature and went on to His Good Friday, when Immortality died and sinners were redeemed; and on further still to His Easter when He rose from the dead for our justification. If Christ be not raised we are yet in our sins—in spite of Bethlehem and the incarnation. But He did rise; and Bethlehem is the earthly beginning of His saving mission. The Word and the Lamb are one.

Thou art the everlasting Word, the Father's only Son;
   God manifestly seen and heard, and Heaven's beloved One.
Worthy, O Lamb of God, art Thou
   That every knee to Thee should bow.

3

THE REALISM OF JESUS

IT IS SOMETIMES suggested that when the Word was made flesh He had an unfair advantage over men. If God indeed dwelt on earth among men His very deity gave Him powers and resources denied to men. Some say that in the fourth gospel, for example, the deity in Jesus is so pronounced that He would have been unable even to feel temptation; or that He is pictured as so divine that He was not human at all. This has been countered by the observation that whereas in the synoptic gospels our Lord's humanity is an obvious fact, in St. John's gospel it is not only a fact but a dogma.

Another criticism comes from an opposite point of view. Religious people—by which is here meant Christian people—are accused of living in a sort of spiritual fairyland, where everything is all right or turns out to be all right. Religion on a good income and with all the comfort of a good home, and the quiet and enjoyment of peaceful surroundings, is a hobby or a practice for those who like it. But if religious people lived the bitter life of the poverty-stricken, the homeless and friendless, and of the under-dog, then they would soon give up their airy-fairy ideas and realize that the life of religion is not what they thought it was. Can a man believe in God, and derive any enjoyment or blessing from his faith, if he has little food, soul-killing work, a squalid home in mean surroundings, and a grinding struggle against the demands of life?

Such is the attitude. The misunderstanding concerns not only the Master's disciples but the Master Himself. He has been regarded as "the pale Galilaean" and a dreamer, out of touch with reality: something of a poet, perhaps, but cut off from the hurly-burly of life; a kind of free-lance monk, a theorizer, endlessly discussing remote questions which never come down to earth.

These are great mistakes. In the first instance insufficient emphasis has been laid on the fact that the Word became *flesh*, with all that that involves. In the second the humanity of Jesus is admitted in principle but its nature is misunderstood. He was no more a mere dreamer than Job, the classical example of a man who will serve God for nought. Jesus was a Man indeed and He served God for nought in the sense that He was not "religious" for the sake of material gain. For Him God was His own reward and the fount of joy. For the joy was that set before Him He endured the cross. . . .

We all know what is meant by "a sheltered life." A man or woman is "sheltered" by the absence of economic need, ignorance of stress and strain, the possession of friends. Political crises mean nothing to them. Even war itself seems to pass them by, and they continue the even tenor of their way. Now we cannot say that such people are not human. They are human; but they have not drunk life's bitterness to the dregs; they have not sounded its depths. Their own life is real for them—as far as it goes. But there are whole areas of life of which they know nothing. To that extent their own lives, human though they are, lack reality. In contrast the life of Jesus manifests a stark realism.

When the Word was made flesh He did not enter a spiritual fairyland; nor did He lead a sheltered life; nor did He live like some characters in the modern detective story: who have their home in a terrible slum but inside the building, hidden from prying eyes, enjoy all the luxuries of oriental magnificence. He took upon Him the seed of Abraham. He Who took upon Him to deliver man and did not despise the virgin's womb, did not despise the language of man or the circumstances of man. He did not become rich Man; He became Man—and at one time had not where to lay His head.

All this is revealed, almost incidentally, in His own words. There is a hard realism in His teaching which shows that He entertained no ideas of the ease and detachment of religion which some assume it to have. He lived in a hard world, as hard in many respects as the world in which we live today, if not harder. If any man doubts that, let him read carefully the Sermon on the Mount as recorded in the fifth, sixth and seventh chapters of Matthew's gospel. As he reads, let him be on the alert to find traces of the rough and seamy side of life. He will be amazed at their abundance.

The Sermon plunges into the bitterness of life at the very beginning. "Blessed are . . ." who? "They that mourn." The meek stand out prominently against a background of the violent; the merciful are in contrast to the pitiless. The pure in heart would not have been singled out unless there had been others impure in thought, feeling and will. The peacemakers cannot work at all unless there are men who are trying to break the peace, and at times succeeding. The persecuted, especially those who are persecuted for righteousness' sake, remind us of the deep divisions in human society. They certainly do not live in fairyland. You who are "the light of the world" would be unnecessary if the world were not in darkness—when evil is afoot.

This is no more than a beginning but we may well pause to ask how our Lord could frame His language in such a way. Who told Him of the evil in men which comes out in their conduct? He Himself was sinless. He was not speaking of what He had done Himself.

This raises the whole question, which goes back as far as Plato, whether knowledge of evil is possible without being personally involved in evil. Plato's opinion is that it is best for men to be intellectually and morally developed to the highest point and then to use their insight. This is correct: the thoroughly bad man cannot appreciate the motives and the conduct of the good man, and the man of mature goodness can see into the character of the bad man. Our Lord recognized evil when He saw it, both its outward act and its inner motive and intention. Nobody informed Him.

But more must be said. This is not only the expression of His insight into character. It is the voice of experience. He is not the impartial observer, watching from his porch the masses of humanity fighting in the street. He has wept with those who weep. He has Himself been the target for men's violence, as on the day in Nazareth when the congregation in the synagogue attempted to throw Him down from the cliff. He has witnessed the evil deeds of men and has penetrated their inner motives. He has experienced the effects of their evil without being a party to it. From both insight and experience He knew what was in man.

Come back to the Sermon on the Mount. There are hypocrites at large; and murderers; and men with murder in their hearts—or anger and resentment. An ominous reference to legal proceedings, not so much criminal as civil lawsuits, carries the threat of judgment and prison. There is a modern ring in the allusion to adultery and divorce. Our Lord's words about "an eye for an eye and a tooth for a tooth"; and about resisting the evil man who has slapped your face: all provide us with a keyhole through which we can look into a world in which man is divided against man and his hand is lifted up against his neighbour—the world in which the Word was made flesh and dwelt among us.

The man who compels you to go a mile was without doubt a

Roman soldier or government agent. It reminds us that Palestine was an "occupied country," like France in 1940-44 or the satellite countries today. The local population was forced into various kinds of service, including the transport of supplies. Dean Alford tells us that the billeting of the Roman soldiers and their horses on the Jews was one kind of compulsion so exercised. Another kind is seen near Golgotha, when they compelled Simon of Cyrene to carry the Lord's cross. It is not unlike the old press-gang days of the British Navy, when a swoop would be made and some innocent young boy carried off to serve at sea. Today we show more politeness: the modern, even the modern civilized state in time of war takes the young man and makes demands on property; but we do it in an orderly manner and speak of conscription, the draft and requisitioning. And religious faith can still flourish in such circumstances. As the journalists and newsmen say, there may be a "story" behind the gospel references to the Roman centurions.

"Doing alms" means what we mean when we speak of giving to charities. It must imply dire poverty with some, or why the need of "charity"? In any case "alms" is related to the word "pity," just as our modern "charity" once meant "love." It is a hard life which excites pity. It is likely that our Lord's family knew poverty at first hand, to judge by the offering of a pair of turtle-doves at His presentation in the Temple. It is even more likely that He Himself gave to the poor.

Religious hypocrites did not prevent the exercise of true religion; and are themselves evidence that our Lord did not live in other than a fallen world. If we are to forgive men their trespasses it is obvious that there can be private wrongs and feuds as well as criminal acts. There seems to have been also something of what we should today call labour troubles. The man who tried to be a slave to two masters hated and despised one of them. Who can deny that some men regard their employer as their natural enemy? There were also "housekeeping" troubles in the world of Jesus. Men were anxious (for this is what is meant by "taking thought") about food and drink and clothes. The breadwinner who had no faith in God had a worrying time.

Our Lord recognized the plain facts of sin. "If you, being evil. . . ." This is no fairyland of pleasant phantasy. It is the awful nightmare of real existence. We are no strangers today to "false prophets." Sometimes they live in the visible church and sometimes in the world. In the world they are recognized today by their "ideologies." In this again our age overlaps the age of Jesus.

He is aware not only of the sphere of politics but of the whole sweep of human nature.

He knew, too, the impact of the forces of nature as well as of human nature. The rain and the consequent overflowing of the dry river-beds, the floods and the winds: the seasonal activities of nature which for many today are summed up in the dread word "hurricane": these are not part of the "comfortable" world which some assert to belong to the religious. And they are not part of the dreamer's idyll. They are the fabric of the life lived by the Word made flesh.

The thirteenth chapter of Mark has been called the synoptic apocalypse. It reveals that our Lord was not unfamiliar with the concept of the catastrophic in nature and of turmoil among men. He speaks of wars and rumours of wars, and the inner disturbance which they bring. He visualizes war or the threat of it on men's very doorsteps. If a man is on the roof, don't stop to go into the house to get anything. Flee! If a man is working in the field, don't go back. The ploughman may have taken off his over-garment because of the heat. He ploughs his furrow, leaving the clothing behind. Don't go back to get it. Flee!

Earthquakes suddenly cause the earth to shiver. Long scarcity issues in famine which gnaws at the vitals of men. Believers are persecuted; brother delivers brother to death; father sends his own child to execution and children do violence to their parents. The modern world saw this kind of bitter division in Nazi Germany, when men—and children—spied on their own families and reported them to the Gestapo. Slavery is evident; the end of the world visualized. Even the weather comes in. "Pray that it may not happen in winter"—or perhaps we should translate "in a storm."

Whether this is to be taken literally or symbolically; or, if both, in what proportion, has long been the subject for debate. We need not stay to dwell on that. The point is that Jesus at the very least knew enough about these calamities to use them as illustrations. He did not live in a beautiful dream. His teaching was the teaching of a realist. He had confidence in God, even though He fully recognized not only human sin but human misery.

Even the sufferings of animals belonged to His world. He observed the falling of a sparrow. We have already referred to the poverty of His family. As a boy He must have watched His mother "house-clean" or "spring-clean" in order to find one lost coin. Who would turn the house upside down today to find twenty-five cents or half a crown except the poor? He knew also about

c

respectable poverty. He had seen those who had come down in the world and He had not missed the unsavoury side of life.

He knew about the apparent unfairness involved in human existence. The Galilaeans had suffered at the hands of Pilate, who had mingled their blood with their sacrifices. It is as if we were present at a Communion Service today and soldiers burst in to slaughter the worshippers: wine and blood together flow. Did the Galilaeans deserve such a fate?

Our Lord knew about the mystery of life and death and of what we should call the problems of workmen's compensation. The tower in Siloam fell on eighteen workmen and killed them. Was it punishment for a life more evil than that of other men? He knew about trade and commerce—goodly pearls, hiring labourers, Galilee on the road to everywhere, and the transport of goods. He faced disease and suffering. He was acquainted with soldiers and tax-collectors. The Roman centurions were laughed at for their hob-nailed shoes, their thick calves and general unkempt roughness but they were the backbone of the Roman army. The rough efficiency of the "strong man in command" is sometimes thought to be far removed from "gentle Jesus, meek and mild," but they came to Him. He knew of brigands and robbers, of "hi-jacking" and the like, and of the beggar who sits at the rich man's gate full of sores, picking up a precarious livelihood from scraps. He knew of a man sold into slavery for debt, together with his wife and children. This is in marked contrast to the modern civilized law of debt. I once kept a man out of prison by paying half a crown a week (say thirty-five cents).

It is clear that any allusion to unreality or fairyland is quite out of place. The world of Jesus was a hard, cold and bitter world. And all this hostility, pain and bitterness was for Him not only observed from the outside but felt from within—without sin. Pre-eminently on the cross did all this woe gather itself together and fall upon His head. Fairyland? Nonsense! He tasted life, with all its problems and agony and death, with all its woe and loneliness. He tasted life and death for every man. The Word was made —flesh.

There is a story told about Baron von Hügel which will sum up for us the central core of the revelation of God in Jesus Christ our Lord. An enlightened employer was explaining to the Baron how he had tried to put Christian principles into operation in his factory. He had taken deep thought for the buildings. The ventilation, we surmise, was adequate and the heating system excellent. There must have been a clinic and a canteen for the workmen. "Welfare" was at the heart of things. No doubt night-classes fed the mind; and a swimming-pool and playing fields promoted a healthy body.

The old Baron listened with impatience. Then came his fierce interruption, telling the employer that he had not even begun to understand the Christian faith. It is not refreshment bars and swimming pools. It is a soul in the presence of God.

We can and do thank God for all the decencies which a Christian public opinion has forced upon employers—from the time of Lord Shaftesbury onwards. But in essence the Baron was right. And it is through this same Jesus that a soul can be in the presence of God, undestroyed and unafraid. "He that hath seen Me hath seen the Father." He, our Lord Jesus Christ, came down from heaven to our earth as it was in its stark actuality, that He might raise His people to heaven in all its beauty and finality, to be for-ever with the Lord. The cost of this inspires the eternal gratitude of the church. For the Word was made—flesh.

4

THE WORD IN THE HEART

SOME YEARS AGO a friend and I were discussing some young men for whom we had a measure of responsibility. I had expressed a certain feeling of disturbance at the manifestation of such religion as they had when my friend turned to me and said with vigour: "What you don't realize is that these men are as much afraid of experience as you are of the Mass."

It was a new thought to me. I had not so far thought of being afraid of the Mass. I repudiate it, for the 31st Anglican Article is essentially sound. The sacrifice of the Mass is in the realm of blasphemous fables and dangerous deceits. And I had not yet thought of any professing Christian being afraid of experience. But confirmation followed. "Do you mean that a man must have a religious experience?" asked a young curate doubtfully. Others, with the omniscience of ecclesiastical youth, have rejected what they are pleased to term the height of subjectivism. Even Dr. Alan Richardson asserts that "the NT writers set no store at all by religious feelings or emotions, and it is impossible to translate 'religious experience' into NT Greek. We are united with Christ in faith through baptism, and whether or not we enjoy an 'experience' is irrelevant."

It is enough at this stage to quote our Lord's words. "These things I have spoken to you that My joy may be in you and your joy fulfilled." (John 15: 11) That joy is hardly irrelevant! It is the fruit of the Spirit (Gal. 5: 22). And "religious experience" can be translated into NT Greek. It has been done.

Why do men turn away from Christian experience? It is partly because they overemphasize the objective. When an Anglo-Catholic friend of mine was converted his mystified friends bemoaned the fact that he had turned from the outer objective offering of the sacrifice to the inner subjective uncertainty. They rely on the objective because the pulse of their own faith is feeble. And I have come with reluctance to believe that many who oppose Christian experience do not know our Lord Jesus Christ in their hearts.

Some words of Bishop Stephen Neill should be salutary here.

There are many ways of describing this experience; I would not wish to insist for a moment on any one terminology. But the experience itself is unmistakable. If you have come by that same way, and entered in through that same narrow door, you will have no difficulty in understanding what I am talking about. If you have not, it is no use pretending that some other experience will do as well. . . . When anyone tells me, as people sometimes do, that he is a once-born Christian, even though I may think that I know what he means, I can only feel sorry.

If this central experience is lacking, you may be able to do many admirable things in the work of the ministry. But one thing will be missing; I think the more sensitive among your people will feel that it is lacking. It is the proclamation of redemption through Christ, with the quiet authority of the man who knows by experience of what he speaks.

I ask you: was Henry VIII a king? Yes, of course, you answer. But he was not characteristically, typically, essentially, a king. It is possible to be a king without being like Henry VIII. There was once a man known as George VI.

I ask you again: was it a game when the spectators started to smash up the stadium and to throw bottles at the referee? Yes, it was a game; but you do not have to assault the referee or ruin the building. Chess and draughts and scrabble are also games.

Was it experience when men spoke in tongues at Pentecost? Yes, it was experience. But Christian experience can occur without tongues.

Was it experience when men groaned and wept and rolled on the ground in paroxysms at the preaching of Wesley and White-field? Yes, it was experience but not essential to experience. You are not compelled so to act.

But we might ask if you are sorry for your sins. That sorrow is experience. And a few tears might not be amiss. Do you mean the General Confession when you say it? That meaning, too, is experience. Notice the words we use: bewail, earnestly, heartily sorry, grievous, intolerable; do these mean nothing to us? If they express what we feel, then there is Christian experience.

Now the Christian faith is a religion of experience. It is not solely experience and is not based entirely on experience. It is based on the Word of God. But unless that Word is unheard, un-read, unknown; unless its promises are disregarded, its call ignored and its Saviour passed by; then it is a Word received; and its reception is Christian experience.

It is sometimes said that we are not saved by experience but by Christ. This may be true but it is a false contrast. We were redeemed by our Lord on the cross apart from our experience; but we are saved by that same Lord *in* experience. The work of grace in men's hearts results in the new creation. Christ's outer work was finished on the cross; His inner work takes place in our hearts, beginning when He takes up permanent residence there. As Paul Bayne quaintly said, "though all of us is a temple for Him, yet the heart is the choir where He properly sitteth."

It was the apostle's prayer that Christ should take up His dwelling in men's hearts—through faith. Notice the significant context. He prays that the Father may give the Ephesians to be mightily strengthened through the coming of His Spirit into the inner man. He desires them to be strengthened. He relates it to power. The apostles received power when the Holy Spirit had come upon them (Acts 1: 8), to be witnesses: "with great power they gave witness or testimony to the resurrection" (Acts 4: 33). Now St. Paul wants the same power to be present in every Christian. The scale is massive. The power is to match the wealth of God's glory. Wealth means that there is plenty of it! But what is His glory?

God's glory means God as He has revealed Himself: His being, His character, His majesty and His might. He has partially disclosed Himself in nature: the heavens declare the glory of God; and revealed Himself yet further in history: He showed Himself glorious in His dealings with Pharaoh (Ex. 14: 4); and He has concentrated His glory in His Son, "the glory" (Jas. 2: 1). All that we see of the glittering starry sky amid the vast realms of space; all that the eye of faith sees in God's mighty act in the Exodus; all the glory of God that we see in Christ: all this is the standard or norm by which to measure the power available to the Christian. It is given through the coming of the Holy Spirit into the believer. That means, in experience, the exercise of faith and the receiving of Christ, for the Holy Spirit is God's method of the presence of Jesus. This, then, is the characteristic experience of the Christian: to receive Christ into the heart and for Him to dwell there, set apart therein as Lord, to call for obedience and to get it.

Take away Christian experience and there remain the objective facts of the life of Christ and His objective atonement, resurrection and ascension. But we have received nothing! But we have not thus learnt Christ. I therefore invite you to consider what is meant by Christ's dwelling in our hearts. And first,

I. *The Beginning of Experience.* At the end of Peter's sermon on the day of Pentecost his congregation was cut to the heart; their conscience was pricked, their soul stabbed awake. "What are we to do, brethren?" came the agonized cry. They were given two duties and a promise. Repent; let each man be baptized in the Name of Jesus Christ; and they would receive the free gift of the Holy Spirit. They received his word and joined the company of those who believe. Their Christian experience had begun.

Christian faith is a compound of belief and trust. The Christian believes what he has been told in the Word—or in the *kerygma*—and he hands himself over in trust or commitment to Christ. He believes that "the Son of God loved me and delivered Himself up for me"; and to the Son of God so described he commits himself. He knows what he is doing and it merits the term experience.

Associated with this is the feeling of deep joy. It has been observed in evangelistic missions that when people are converted they know a throbbing joy and deep content with Christ. They have not merely oozed into church membership without commitment; they have found Christ, received Him by the Spirit Whose fruit is joy. Sometimes there is a background of privilege and sometimes one of felt sin. The man who could beat all comers in fleshly confidence abandoned his qualifications. "We, Jews by extraction (and not by naturalization) and not sinners belonging to the gentiles, and knowing that a man is not justified from works of law but through faith in Christ Jesus, even we (even!) set our faith in Christ Jesus, so that we might be justified from faith in Christ and not from works of law. . . ." Even we! This is almost sublime. For "we" were the people of privilege. To us had been committed the oracles of God. Ours was the adoption and the glory and the covenants and the legislation and the worship and the promises. Ours were the patriarchs and from us came the Christ according to the flesh, Who is God over all, blessed for ever.

Always in conversion there is a background of sin. But with some its hue is darker, blacker than deepest night. "Do you not know that the unrighteous will not inherit the Kingdom of God? . . . Neither fornicators nor idolators nor adulterers nor the effeminate nor homosexuals nor thieves nor extortioners nor drunkards nor revilers nor the rapacious will inherit the Kingdom of God. *And such were some of you*; but you washed, you were sanctified, you were justified in the Name of the Lord Jesus Christ and in the Spirit of our God." These "some" knew the meaning of Christian experience. And the others, involved in sins less gross, would know that from which they had been saved before they thus sinned. Their relief and gratitude that they had first met with Christ was Christian experience likewise. In the one group Christ in the heart expelled the sinful demons; in the other He prevented their entry. Thus they began their Christian life. We pass on to

II. *The Growth of Experience.* The new Christian is nourished in his faith by the Word of God, read and heard; by prayer and fellowship. He is not merely "prayed over" by the minister; he prays himself, in private and in company. Deep within his heart there is something which must have an outlet, which bursts forth in season and out of season. We cannot but speak the things which we have seen and heard, said the apostles. And now Lord, prayed the church, look upon their threats and give to Thy servants—give what? A discharge from their spiritual responsibility? A deliverance from all danger? A perpetual freedom from persecution? No; give to Thy servants to go on speaking Thy Word with all boldness. Note, with *all* boldness; not half-heartedly but up to the very limit.

After Stephen's martyrdom the scattered church—without the apostles—went right on, spreading the good news of the Word and of the Lord Jesus. The hand of the Lord was with them. Barnabas, full of the Holy Spirit and of faith, recognized the grace of God and rejoiced, bidding all the converts to hold fast to the Lord with purpose of heart. Christian experience is growing and deepening.

With these men it was an outward thrust, a spontaneous though obedient constant evangelistic drive. It was true of St. Paul though he showed also an inner cultivation of spirit and sought for a growth in experience. It was not for its own sake and certainly not experience in the abstract. He yearned to know Christ more and more. What was gain for me I have counted loss for Christ's sake. Yes, and not only that: I consider everything to be loss because of the surpassing worth of the knowledge of Christ Jesus my Lord, for Whose sake I have suffered the loss of everything and count it but garbage that I may gain Christ and be found in Him . . . to know Him and the power of His resurrection and the fellowship of His sufferings.

Here is St. Paul thinking and feeling. He looks at all his gains, at his all, and gladly lets everything go. To know Christ is better. He thinks and compares and assesses. To know Christ is everything. To know Him surpasses everything that men value and for that he is prepared to lose everything and to suffer.

Someone will assert that such an experience is for the few. It may be enjoyed by the few but it is for the many. This is life eternal, that they grow in the knowledge of Thee the only true God and Jesus Christ Whom Thou didst send. Take away Christian experience and you take away eternal life. Christians are not like this, you say? Then they ought to be; and we who are ministers ought to set the example.

In our emphasis on the corporate life of the church we tend to forget these basic facts. But without such personal knowledge of Christ; without Him in the hearts of believing men the corporate church is no more than an amorphous mass, a mere sociological entity. Whatever the characteristics of the church as a whole, it is made up of individual believing men. *Thou* art no longer *a* slave but *a* son.

Christ dwells in our hearts through the Holy Spirit, and the Spirit testifies that we are sons. In proof that we are sons God sent forth the Spirit of His Son into our hearts, shouting Abba, Father. The Spirit shouts, as the apostle tells the Galatians. You received the spirit of sonship, he tells the Romans, in Whom we shout Abba, Father. The Spirit shouts. We shout. This theological distinction is blurred in Christian experience. In our hearts who is shouting? the Spirit or we ourselves? The Spirit Himself testifies with our spirit that we are children of God. Taught by the Spirit we shout Abba, Father. Charles Wesley understood this:

> If now the Witness were in me,
> Would He not testify of Thee
> In Jesus reconciled?
> And should I not with faith draw nigh,
> And boldly Abba, Father! cry,
> And know myself Thy child?

We cannot but speak. We have purpose of heart. We know Christ and set such knowledge above everything. We seek to know Him more and more. We are no longer slaves but sons. We have the witness of the Spirit.

This is Christian experience at its deeper levels. Is it irrelevant? Do you despise it? Is it worth nothing to you to know that you are a child of God? Have you no wish to know our Lord more and more? Have you the witness of the Spirit? If you are out of sympathy with all this, look into your own heart: does Christ dwell there permanently? Is your faith a vital trust or a dull acquiescence in the so-called spiritual nature of man? Do you preach this—or just turn the handles of a liturgical barrel-organ? Is the love of God shed abroad in your heart?

There is yet one higher peak. We reach upward now to

III. *The Crown of Experience.* Nearly seventy years ago James Denney read two volumes of Newman's sermons. He found desperately little in them. "He knows man very well, but he does not know God at all. There is a mixture in them of cowardice, almost, towards God, and domineering toward men. . . ." How different is the apostle to the gentiles! In Christ and through faith in Him we have boldness and access with confidence: a bold and confident approach to the living God. This is the authentic mark of those who believe the Word of God written, interpret it through the illumination of the Holy Spirit, trust in Jesus Christ and His shed blood and know God in the intimacy of the secret place. This is not a cheap familiarity and irreverence; it is the logical and practical outcome of the experience of sonship.

Its ripe fruit will be seen on the day of judgment. With us love is perfected in this, that we have boldness in the day of judgment. Why not? Already, in this world, we also are as Christ was. This does not mean that we claim for ourselves a character and a goodness equal to His and produced by our own efforts. It does mean that in Christ we have an access to the Father as sure and certain as His. God has given us an *eternal* encouragement, according to St. Paul. And if we are nervous on that dread Day, the same Christ Who encouraged His people on their earthly road will be present to remind them that He has bought them with His blood.

Some people, especially those of the "catholic" persuasion, look upon such confidence as presumption. Protestants see in it one of the privileges of believers. All that we have from God is a "privilege," given to us by His mercy and received by grace and not as of right. Confidence is not a special privilege; in the New Testament faith it is a plain fact. It takes God at His Word, claims nothing for human merit or achievement, believes the promises of God and trusts Christ utterly. This is the crown of Christian experience and it is open to every disciple.

Such, in outline, is what happens to men when Christ dwells in their hearts. It has certain lessons for us and makes certain claims upon us. We must therefore give some attention to

IV. *The Implications of Experience.* The minister of the Word of God, as a preacher, must not be a theorist who lectures on the exegesis of the New Testament but has not himself tasted its blessings. He must preach the Word as he has known it in his own

experience. This is not a question of starving his congregation
because the preacher's experience is so thin. Preach the Christ you
know; and constantly deepen your knowledge of Christ by study
of the Word written.

The preacher, in fact, like the scribe discipled to the Kingdom
of Heaven, brings forth from his treasure things new and old. The
"old," which has stood the test of time, is the abiding Word,
written and living; the "new" is his own insight into the meaning, his own knowledge of its truth, his own experience of its
nourishment and power. He comes to his people fresh from
personal converse with the living God in Christ, available in the
Word written and present by the Holy Spirit.

St. Paul illustrates this admirably. He speaks of the "Father of
mercies and God of all encouragement, Who encourages us in all
our affliction, so that we may be able to encourage others in every
affliction by means of the encouragement with which we ourselves are encouraged by God." From his own experience he
addresses himself to the experience of others, to confirm it, to
correct it or to create it. Do you preach from your mind or from
your mind and heart?

Does Christ dwell in your heart? If not, you will lack that
authentic sign of the messenger of God. Open the door to Him,
for behold He stands there, knocking. He does dwell in your
heart? Then preach Him as you know Him, and ever learn Him
that you may continue to preach Him. This is vital to our ministry
and to the health of the church; and indeed to the salvation of
men. One of the sad—and disturbing—features of many religious
books is that the authors do not seem to write as men who know
Christ; and when they stand in the pulpit they give the same
melancholy impression.

It is fashionable nowadays to speak much of "dialogue." I see
the motive and have some sympathy. But ultimately this is not
our method, certainly not in the pulpit. "Go, tell" is what we
have been told to do: proclaim the gospel as a herald. As John the
Baptist preached, certain that he was the forerunner of the Christ;
so the preacher is the forerunner of the Saviour Who will enter
every believing heart in the pew. Tell! not discuss. There is no
other Name under heaven given among men whereby we must
be saved: it is a unique, given and compulsory Name. God commands men that all should everywhere repent. Go tell!

We persuade men, said St. Paul. What he did to the Corinthians
to vindicate his personal integrity and apostleship he did to all
men, Jews and Greeks, to win them to Christ. We persuade men.

Do we? If we do, it is because we are so commanded in God's Word; because God has laid His hand upon us; and because Christ dwelling in our hearts thrusts outwards in our words: in a new sense "He cannot be hid."

We encourage; we tell; we persuade: that is the overflow of a heart in which Christ dwells. Will the apostle's prayer be answered in your case? He prays that the Father may give you. . . . The offer is there and it is open. God has done His part; it remains for you to do yours. Fling wide the gates!

5

THE WORK OF CHRIST

IN THE CREDAL burst of praise known as the *Te Deum Laudamus* there is a direct address to our Lord Jesus Christ: "Thou art the King of Glory: O Christ. Thou art the everlasting Son: of the Father. When Thou tookest upon thee to deliver man. . . ." The last clause is an apt statement of the purpose of the incarnation. The Word was made flesh in order to deliver man. That is to say, Christ came to deal with a situation. Man, as man, is under obligation to render certain duties to God. Man, as sinner, will not and cannot. The "situation" is the fact of sin.

It is sometimes said that Christ would have become incarnate even if man had not sinned. This may or may not be true. It is pure speculation. And it is not particularly helpful. At best it emphasizes the eternal purpose of the incarnation but it runs the risk of getting Christian doctrine out of proportion. We must not emphasize the incarnation as such, as if the fact of incarnation by itself could "deliver man." The New Testament does not speak of "the Word of the manger" but "the Word of the Cross." Calvary is more than Bethlehem raised to a lofty and lonely peak. It is the place where He Who was born in Bethlehem redeemed the world. And the world needed to be redeemed. Wherever man appears in the New Testament it is as a sinner: either just a sinner or a sinner on whom the saving hands of Christ have been laid. And Christ is likewise shown not only as the incarnate Lord but as the Saviour.

Man, as an individual, is a sinner and each man belongs to a sinful human race. There is a solidarity in sin. If ever any safe prediction can be made it can surely be made of every infant born: he will be a sinner. In all of history there has been but One sinless Person. "All have sinned" says the New Testament in a context of the Adamic race. "All have sinned" it says again in a context of faith in Jesus Christ, and faith is individually exercised.

This is not a welcome doctrine today, and some pulpits (as well as some pews) are strangely silent about it. It is true that in some

quarters there is clamour for social justice, which some have con-
strued as an implied repentance for our social sins of omission.
This is sound as far as it goes. We may not be the massive
industrialist who exploited his workmen or the trader who took
advantage of the simple native. But we were involved in the
social system which permitted it and did not raise our voices in
protest early enough. But this does not go deep enough. It puts
the stress on sinful solidarity; but "I, even I," am a sinful man.
We may be like one another in our common sinfulness—but
selfishness, covetousness, hypocrisy, jealousy and impurity of
thought belong to the individual.

Not all sins are criminal and not all sins are gross. There are
sinful men who are not murderers or adulterers in act. Sin is
ultimately a characteristic of the mind and heart.

Sin is, first, an implicit denial by man that he is a creature. He
was created by God and he owes his existence to God. He persists, however, in behaving as if he were himself the creator. As a
creature he is dependent but he acts as if he were self-sufficient.
He takes—or tries to take—from the world all that he wants. We
admit that God said "I have given you. . . ." We admit that God
ordained man to subdue the earth and to have dominion. But man
thinks nothing of this. He proceeds as if God had not spoken. As
created and dependent man, he is under obligation to obey God.
On the contrary he is indifferent to his duty or even opposes the
existence of God.

As creature, then, he acts as if he were the creator. As dependent
he behaves as if he were self-sufficient and takes *what* he wants.
As under obligation he acts as if he were free, and he takes *how* he
wants. He ignores his spiritual duty and withholds from God the
thanksgiving and worship which are His due. He fails to give
glory to God. He ignores his moral duty. This does not mean that
every man is obviously a brute beast. Even sinners love those who
love them and do good to those who do good to them. There is
within the order of creation such a thing as family love: not all
husbands are bullies and not every wife is faithless. But man, left
to himself, is essentially sinful and sinful means godless.

Not all men are aggressive atheists; but they may be practical
atheists. They may accept the fact of God's existence but they live
as if He did not exist. They suppress His truth by ignoring it.
They may even believe in some form of immortality but they are
immersed in the details of the earthly journey. We should note
here our Lord's significant words when He compared the days of
the Son of Man with the days of Noah and of Lot. Men were

eating and drinking, marrying and giving in marriage, buying and selling, planting and building. There is nothing inherently sinful in any of these occupations but their sequel is doom. Why is this?

The answer is that men were absorbed in them. It is a remarkable picture of a secular civilization, very much like our own. The activities are part of the life of men; but men have made them the whole. They have no time for God; no interest in Him; no sense of gratitude and none of loyalty. The activities are innocent; but the men are not.

It is even possible for men to be virtuous sinners. Their lives may be outwardly clean; they may have the welfare of their staff at heart; in games they may play fairly and follow the noblest sporting traditions; their civic influence may be wholesome and they may be the enemies of all graft. They may shun the ruthlessness of competitive business and care for the poor. They may never quarrel with their friends and may have no enemies. But by their godlessness they are sinners.

Such men may be excellent logicians and be proud of "thinking things out" on their own. But not only are their reasonings in vain; they themselves as thinkers are in vain. For, as St. Paul tells us, their heart is unintelligent. They have a mental and moral blind spot. They cannot understand the spiritual. The "natural" man does not receive the things of the Spirit of God. He regards them as foolishness and he cannot grasp them because they are spiritually discerned. Even the Word of the Cross is foolishness to them because "the god of this age" has blinded their thoughts. They affirm their own wisdom; in fact they are themselves making a claim without foundation: they have become fools.

To say this is not to hurl ecclesiastical abuse at those who are outside the church. It is a statement of sober fact. For the godless —the secular—is limited in his thought to the evidence available to him. He completely ignores the fact of the living God.

In this connection we have not given enough attention to the faith of Abraham, at any rate in its relation to the method of the scientist and the general scientific atmosphere of today. The scientist, quite properly, adopts as a working assumption the uniformity of nature and tries to discover natural laws. As far as it goes this is not unscriptural for the Bible recognizes an order in nature. "While the earth remaineth, seedtime and harvest, and cold and heat, and summer and winter, and day and night shall not cease." This is a simple statement but it establishes a principle. For practical purposes the scientist works within a closed order and in his investigations he no more expects to find the miraculous or the supernatural than a detective admits the hand of the devil to explain a murder. But if the scientist is a believing man he believes that God works outside the order of nature as well as inside. This is the implication of the story of Abraham.

Here is a married couple, both in a ripe old age. The possibility of children is long passed. Old people do not have children! But God promised them a son and a son was born. "By faith even Sarah herself received power—to meet (*eis*) the emission of semen, and so—to conceive, even though she had passed the time of life." And "from one man, and dead at that," came a posterity as numerous as the stars of heaven and the sand of the sea-shore. Now in a strictly scientific atmosphere Abraham and Sarah would have been told to take no notice of the promise. "These things do not happen." The Bible says that they do, and it is because God is the living God, free to act as He wills. Abraham was empowered by faith and it was reckoned to him as righteousness.

Now man as a sinner is unintelligent and foolish because he will insist on living within a closed order; he will take eternal decisions on the basis of the immediately available evidence. He regards himself as rational and Abraham as irrational. But he is guilty of distortion and changes the truth of God for a lie. He has the impertinence to impose a qualifying examination before he will admit God to his knowledge, and the even greater impertinence of not giving a pass mark. But it is he himself who has failed, having what St. Paul called "a reprobate mind." The result is moral ruin.

This may show itself in sins too evil even to be mentioned. On the other hand it may not "show itself" in the outer, grosser sins at all. But there will be an inner, atheistic Phariseeism. The "virtuous sinner" is a whited sepulchre, marvellously sculptured and beautiful to look upon; but inside are dead men's bones. For he has set himself up in opposition to God and in rebellion against Him. He may not have the religious cultus of the heathen. But he is an idolator. Pride is idolatry and the sinner worships himself.

All this can be illustrated in a variety of ways. Man is a passenger in a Greyhound coach who takes over the driver's seat—and will not keep to the route. He is employed in a store and insinuates himself into the position not only of the manager who directs it but of the president who owns it. He is given the use of a house and he sells it—and pockets the proceeds. He is the treasurer of a charitable institution and he deflects all the contributions into his own banking account. He is a minister of God who not only preaches false doctrine but sets up a new denomination with himself as its god. In all such imperfect pictures we see the essence of sin: it is God-less self. And it is self enthroned against its only Benefactor, a sordid, surly and caddish rebellion with treachery at its heart, and the meaning of loyalty unknown.

What does God think of this? If we are to give an answer we must know something of the character of God. It may be summed up in the word "righteousness."

The Hebrew people tended to see this in terms of black and white. If a man were righteous, then he was in the right; if he were not righteous he was in the wrong. It was as clear-cut as if a decision had been given by a judge in court. (This is what is meant when the term "forensic" is used.) With sinful men righteousness means "to be in the right with God" in spite of their sin; with God righteousness means "to be in the right absolutely." There is of course a savour of the ethical for under the Law a man would hardly be in the right with God if he were wicked.

"Lord, who shall sojourn in Thy tabernacle? Who shall dwell in Thy holy hill? He that walketh uprightly, and worketh righteousness, and speaketh truth in his heart. He that slandereth not with his tongue, nor doeth evil to his friend. . . ." "Blessed are they that keep judgment, and he that doeth righteousness at all times." "Woe unto him that buildeth his house by unrighteousness, and his chambers by injustice; that useth his neighbour's service without wages, and giveth him not his hire. . . ."

Thus God is in the right absolutely. He is utter moral perfection. This is an aspect of the divine holiness. God is separate from, and above, all that is not God. He is unapproachable except on His own terms. He is supreme and intends to remain so, the ground of His own existence and the standard of His own character. In Him is all power and all moral excellence.

Man as a sinner is an affront to the living God. His rebellion is a defiance of God's authority, a misuse of His power and a negation of His moral goodness. It is an idolatry which offends, for it sets up another god; and God will not give His own glory to another. It bites the very hand that blessed it. Unchecked, it would undermine and blow to pieces the validity of absolute goodness. It is disobedience to the fount of goodness; it is evil and alien.

God in His righteousness re-acts against the sin of man. He is

D

opposed to it and hostile to it. The face of the Lord is against them that do evil. The Bible calls this "wrath." It is not arbitrary or irrational; it is not the outburst of temper caused by frustration nor is it merely human passion raised to its highest power. There is a prophetic use of such passionate terms as "fury" for the sake of vividness but it is a rich anthropomorphism which needs interpretation. It is not malicious nor does it just seek revenge. It is the intolerance—the true intolerance—of all evil, and it is the affirmation and upholding of the right and good.

Such a re-action is a personal attitude in the living God. He may work through moral laws in a moral universe just as He works through natural laws in the natural universe but ultimately His wrath is His displeasure with sinners and a determination that unrighteousness shall not be enthroned. When God's attitude is put into act we have an observable situation—as Paul showed in the first chapter of his letter to the Romans. The principle of retribution which is a necessity in a moral universe is at work in the affairs of the individual and of the nation and human race.

"Wrath" is an eschatological term and refers to that final vindication of the good which is associated with the end of the age. It is anticipated during the present age when God sees fit to bring home men's sin to them.

Now if God's attitude to sin and sinners is on the lines which have been indicated, what is He to do about the situation? In theory He can destroy the whole universe of sinful men; or He can be indifferent and ignore them and their sin; or He can pardon them by a universal amnesty with no questions asked; or He can deal with the situation.

But if God loves sinners how can He begin by destroying them? If in Him righteousness and moral excellence is enthroned He can neither ignore the sin nor pardon it by His mere fiat. This would be inconsistent; would be against his "conscience"; and would be a practical denial of the supremacy of right. Goodness itself would be eternally besmirched. In His love and mercy He determined to uphold His righteousness and at the same time to express His love.

So we come to the heart of the gospel, the plan of salvation. There are men who have nothing but ridicule for this expression. But a church which does not refuse the use of the term *logos* is in no position to object to the word "plan."

God planned to maintain His attitude of opposition to sin and at the same time to reveal His love of sinners. He has not gone back on anything that He has said or done. The face of the Lord is against sinners—and always will be. But in Christ He is "for sinners."

He sent His Son, Jesus Christ our Lord, for us men and our salvation. He lived a life of perfect obedience. Not a single moral flaw is to be found in Him. And on the cross He offered that life, without blemish and without spot, to God in a sacrificial death. He died for our sins; He bore our sins.

Some people say that they accept the fact of the atonement but deny any knowledge of its meaning. Admittedly Calvary was wrought in the dark. But God has revealed its meaning to us. There may indeed be depths in the cross which we have not yet penetrated but with the New Testament epistles before us we cannot say that we know nothing.

In the cross God judged sin. Jesus our Lord bore God's judgment. He stood where men should stand; He bore the judgment which they should bear. The inflexible divine opposition to sin was concentrated on Him. He stood under the wrath. There are events in history which can be regarded as the wrath of God, but His greatest wrath is seen when He turns away from men. "Then My anger shall be kindled against them in that day, and I will forsake them, and I will hide My face from them. . . ." This is precisely what happened in the cross. "My God, My God, why hast Thou forsaken Me?"

At this point certain precautionary statements have to be made. It is not that the saving Son persuaded an angry Father; it is not that the Son embodies love and the Father justice. The Father out of love for sinners sent His Son. The Father needed no persuasion to act for the salvation of men. And the Son stands for justice and righteousness just as the Father does. He took man's place in the dock but agreed with the Father about the heinousness of the charge. We must not suppose that the Father Who spared not His own Son refused to save until He had "taken it out" of an innocent Man. Such an idea suggests a separation between Father and Son. Without subscribing to patripassionism we can say that in a very real sense God inflicted His wrath upon Himself in the Person of His Son. The Son suffered a break in communion with His Father—not a metaphysical disunion but an experiential one. Who can say what it meant to the Father to lose the fellowship of His Son? Nor was the Father personally displeased with His Son. At all times and pre-eminently when He hung forsaken on the cross the Lord was "My Beloved Son in Whom I am well pleased." He stood under the wrath only as He stood in our place. In that dread hour of utter isolation, when Father and Son were separated because the Father withdrew Himself from the Son, Father and Son were one in mutual love, in love for sinners and in their saving purpose for men.

Christ died for sinful men. The righteousness of God is maintained and perfect goodness is unsullied. The Father is free to pardon. We are not saved illegitimately or immorally, by a dodge or a fiat. Salvation is possible because God's righteousness is intact.

Various illustrations have been used in the attempt to expound these deep things of God. There is the picture of the court of law, suggested by justice and justification; the institution of slavery, where the slave's redemption or liberation by a money payment points to the cost of man's salvation; and the sacrificial system in which the blood atones. All such categories have their place and value and no doubt they overlap in men's experience. But in understanding what Christ has done for sinful men it is vital to remember that God's hostility to sinners as such, His wrath, has been brought to an end by His own provision in Christ and His cross. The primary reference of the cross is to God. It is not merely that we see the love of God shining forth in splendour from the cross. We do see it, but this is not basic. The sacrifice for sin was an offering of the obedient life to God, and if nobody ever believed the gospel it would still be true that God in His righteousness has been satisfied in the death of His Son.

God, then, is free to forgive. How does He do it? Or what are His "terms"? They are very simple in their application. It is through faith in Jesus Christ Who died for us. If a man in response to the preaching of the cross "hands himself over in trust to Christ" he is accepted by God and is forgiven all his sins. This is St. Paul's celebrated doctrine of justification by faith alone. When a man has faith in Christ he is justified, that is, he is accounted just or righteous. There has been a long debate between Roman Catholics and Protestants on the meaning of "justify." Does it mean "make righteous" or "deem righteous"? This depends on whether in interpreting "righteous" we emphasize "being in the right with God," which is a matter of status; or whether we emphasize "righteous in character." When we put our faith in Christ God "makes us right with Him." In this sense we have to use the word "make" because we really are right with God. Theologians sometimes say that justification is eschatological. This means that when a man first puts his faith in Christ the very Day of Judgment is brought forward to the present moment of faith and the Judge gives a verdict of "not guilty." He is acquitted. Through his faith God has made him acceptable to Himself.

But if we emphasize "righteous in character" we must not use the word "make." God deems or accounts the believer righteous. He does not make him virtuous at once in response to his faith and therefore accept him as a good man. It is helpful here to consider one of the apostle's figures of speech. Paul speaks of "putting on Christ." It is a metaphor from clothes, as when we say: "It is cold today; I will put on my overcoat." Now when we come home and tell our family that "I saw Smith today" they know what we mean though we are not strictly accurate. We did not really see Smith; we saw his clothes—and enough of him, his face, to recognize him. It is like that with "putting on Christ." When God looks at believing men there are two factors to be remembered. He does not see the men; He sees their clothes— Christ. But He sees enough of them to identify them. He sees their face. "The Lord knoweth them that are His." Thus comes about the double exchange. Christ on the cross has been made sin for us; through our faith we have been made the righteousness of God in Him. Our sin has been laid on Him; His righteousness is imputed to us.

Some comments must be made on this by way of explanation. Our faith is not a "work" which deserves recognition by God; it is not a work of merit. This would be justification by works coming in by a back—or at least a side—door. Our faith does not "count" or contribute to a store of merit by which we deserve salvation. It is all of grace and faith is the manner of receiving it.

Objection is sometimes made to the doctrine of justification by faith on the ground that it savours of a legal fiction which even God, as righteous, is not at liberty to adopt. Even God cannot say that black is white. This can be answered either by saying that "justify" means "make right with God," where there is no legal or any other kind of fiction, because in status before God the believer really is right with Him and acceptable to Him in Christ. Or we can take up the challenge of "fiction." Cannot God say that black is white? Cannot He treat the bad man as good? Surely it is the very glory of God that in His grace and mercy He looks on all of us who believe, bad as we are, *as if* we were good. "Legal" is not quite the word, even though it is but an illustration. "Fiction" is not pre-possessing but let us face it. If my neighbour in a fit of temper or in a cold rage deliberately smashes my windows, lets the air out of my tyres, and slanders me before dozens of my acquaintances and then in genuine sorrow comes and apologizes and wants to be a genuine friend once more; and if I forgive him; then we resume the friendship at the point where it broke off—*as if* the outrage had never happened. If we like to use the word what is this but fiction? He did smash my windows —and my reputation. But all that is as if it had never been. As a matter of fact "as if" is a sound expression for weighty New Testament teaching. "We died with Christ." Did we? We were not there. When in repentance we turn to Christ and trust Him, the self-asserting *ego* is replaced by an *ego* which repudiates self and hands it over to the Lord. Self is, so to speak, crucified. It is *as if* I in my egotism had died with Christ. And in any case the "legal fiction" is not quite pure. The unrighteous man who is accounted righteous may have no righteousness or ethical virtues of his own but in his act of faith, of giving himself to Christ, he sides with righteousness. It is thus not a question of God calling a bad man good who has no intention of being anything but bad. He has heard the call of Christ and he knows that he must henceforth walk in His steps. In believing he has started in principle though at this stage he has achieved nothing.

The faith through which we are justified thus initiates a new relationship with God. The believer is accepted by God in Christ for ever. His continuing faith continues the new relationship. He is a forgiven man, acceptable to God. Thus justification is both a past act and a present experience. When a man first puts his faith in Christ he is justified; he is accepted by God. His status with God—"no longer a slave but a son"—is for ever dependent on his faith in Christ. The result is that though the Christian's justification is "past history" it is not merely past history. The new relationship to God in grace is a continuing experience in the present, dependent on his continuing faith. And once justified the believer goes on to turn the gold bullion of justification into the coinage of sanctification.

It may be helpful here to consider the confession of sin uttered in private and in public by those who use such prayers as the General Confession. They may be appropriate, it may be argued, for those who are repenting and believing for the first time. With sin confessed so seriously, is there no thought given for Christian maturity and growth in grace? The answer may be given by an illustration.

Those whose work is occupied with legal documents know that deeds are sometimes executed but not witnessed. The situation has to be remedied. Somebody has to sign to record the fact that he has witnessed the signature. I once asked an examining officer what guarantee he had that a man who signed *now* as a witness had really seen the original act of signing *then*. His reply was interesting. In such cases, he said, the man in question goes over his original signature with a dry pen. The witness can then sign that he has witnessed the signature.

I know nothing of the legality of this but as an illustration it is helpful. When a man first puts his faith in Christ he is, as it were, signing his name to record his allegiance to Christ. When later he expresses his faith—perhaps many times—by saying the General Confession, he is not putting his first faith in Christ and is not being justified all over again. He is going over his original work "with a dry pen." All those Christians, already born again, who in evangelistic missions and the like "re-affirm their faith" are doing the same thing.

The same may be said about certain services organized by enterprising ministers. Some have an "annual marriage service" in which fifty or more married couples come to church and the clergyman goes through the marriage service. The congregation contains people who have been married five, ten, fifteen, twenty or more years. They are not "being married all over again." They are re-affirming their pledge and their mutual love. They are going over their former signature with a dry pen.

So it is even with the mature Christian. He confesses not only the sins of yesterday but his sin generally. He is not a sinner coming home to God for the first time. He is a sinful son (for we are all unprofitable servants) not only confessing the sins of today but re-affirming his justifying faith. All his continuing Christian life, with its growth in grace and its sanctification, is dependent on whether he is acceptable to God; and he is so acceptable, not because now he is a better man than he was when he was converted but because God still accepts him through his faith in Christ.

Thus in the cross our Lord did His "outer" work. He is the propitiation for our sins and God is willing to receive sinners—even if no sinner in the world ever came to Christ. This is the objective atonement, done for us and apart from us and independently of us. His "inner" work begins in our hearts when we first exercise faith in Jesus; and that new relationship to God in Him is in virtue of the cross and of our justifying faith. That is why St. Paul preached "the word of the cross" and determined to know nothing save Jesus Christ and Him crucified.

There are those who do not understand the meaning of this concentration. They think that either every sermon must be evangelistic or must deal with the crucifixion. In a sense every sermon should be evangelistic in that the preacher should preach for a verdict. But suppose on some special occasion he is preaching to believers? He will not be evangelistic in the more restricted sense though he should still preach the Word of God. He may make an appeal in case unbelievers are present but in the main he will deal with "the deep things of God" appropriate not to the natural, carnal or immature man but to the mature in Christ.

Further "the word of the cross" is not the same as "the word of the crucifixion." Unbelieving men could—and did—witness the crucifixion. But the cross is more than the crucifixion. It is *the crucifixion plus a sequel and a meaning.* The sequel is the resurrection; the meaning is the atonement. That is why in the prayer called the General Thanksgiving "we bless Thee . . . *above all* for Thine inestimable love in the redemption of the world by our Lord Jesus Christ."

The apostle's concentration on the cross was partly evangelistic, in order that justifying faith might be created; but it was also pastoral and theological. The "cross" is thus not a gramophone record, to be played and re-played without change. It is a dye into which all doctrines and all experience must be dipped. It is here that the modern pulpit so signally fails. We have sermons on creation, on behaviour, on "iron curtains" of various kinds like those between East and West, black and white, rich and poor, upper and lower class or Jew and Gentile; but not always is each sermon or each doctrine related to the cross.

Suppose we are thinking of creation. The doctrine of creation must be dipped into the dye of the cross. The forces of nature are tremendous and even if a man does not believe that matter as such is evil he might be tempted to dwell on the evil in some of the events of nature and allow them to colour his thought of God. Nature is red in tooth and claw; wild animals tear one another to pieces; men, even civilized men, suffer from the lightning, the avalanche, the volcano, the hurricane and the earthquake. It is one thing to say that all these natural powers derive from God. But Who is God? And what is He like? The answer is that He is the God and Father of our Lord Jesus Christ, Whom He sent for us men and for our redemption. God's Son suffered for us on the cross; God sent Him to do it; and God was in Christ. Thus behind all the convulsions and mysteries of creation we see the God Whom we know in His Son—in Christ crucified for us. Amid all our perplexities about the behaviour of the created world there are yet words for God: the word of the cross.

Or think of our doctrine—and practice—of prayer. It must not be unrelated to the cross. At this point the church breaks with all who believe that man is autonomous. Politically we speak, and rightly speak, of autonomous or self-governing peoples; but they are self-governing solely in relation to other nations or races. It is wrong to apply autonomy to humanity in the sight of God. There are men who assert that man can stand on his own feet in the presence of God and that man is utterly independent of any being other than himself; independent even of the work of Christ. But man cannot stand on his own feet; he certainly cannot come into God's presence unaided, independent. Only One has opened the Kingdom of Heaven to all believers. Apart from Him the way is barred.

Now when we come to God in prayer we do not come with self-assertiveness, like the inverted snob who is always claiming that "I am as good as you are." We come in humility, for we have no rights to come at all, apart from Christ. All God's gifts, including the answers to prayer, are given to us in Christ. "He that spared not His own Son but delivered Him up for us all: will He not lavish everything upon us also—with Him?" Our every prayer is through Jesus Christ our Lord. It is through Him that we are able to approach the Father; it is through Him that we are encouraged to approach the Father; and from Him we infer that if God has given His Son for us—and to us—He has given us everything in principle. All the glittering wonders of heaven's storehouse are open to our asking.

Prayer is of course part of our moral and spiritual life. It is its discipline and its delight. Through prayer and prayerful reading of God's Word written we grow in grace and holiness. We become holy by obedience and Christian obedience is well linked with gratitude. Why should we obey God? We should obey because we are His—by creation; by redemption; by conversion; by His keeping power; and by His promise of our glorious destiny. When we are converted our eyes are opened. We see what our Lord has done for us in the cross. We see that God, the Father of the crucified Jesus, made us, redeemed us, caused us to be born again, rules us and leads us by His providence and is with us in fellowship, and in Christ promises us a destiny beyond our imagination. Can the disciple, realizing that the cross is central in the love of God and in Christian men's experience, withhold his obedience? Gratitude for the cross is an ingredient in our growing holiness. Without the shedding of blood there is no remission; and without the cross there is no deep sanctification.

And the cross must not be absent from our doctrine of "last things." Christ being raised from the dead dies no more. But He is always the Lord of the cross. "We preach Christ crucified" says St. Paul. "Crucified" is a perfect participle, and the perfect tense can always be re-interpreted with a present meaning. "Having been crucified" suggests not "He is now dead" but "He possesses now the experience of being crucified" and better still "He now bears the scars of the cross." At the judgment believers do not come to condemnation because they have already been acquitted. "There is now no condemnation to those who are in Christ Jesus." The very rewards given to those who merit the "Well done, good and faithful servant" flow from the grace of the cross. Associated with the Judgment is the Second Advent, which is itself the return of the crucified and risen Jesus for His own. And in heaven itself the old title used in John's gospel is not given up or forgotten. There, the cynosure of all eyes and the focus of all hearts, is the Lamb as it had been slain.

It is fitting that the Lord should still be known as the Lord of the cross. For He was the only One worthy to open the book of history and destiny and to break the seals. The meaning of history and light on destiny is revealed in the cross. For the cross determines the destiny of every man, though the road may fork. God's purpose was and is to get Him a people for His Name, and all who trust in His Son join His concourse of joyous disciples, a vast throng which no man can number. Those who refuse the gospel and go to their own place will have rejected the cross. But it will have triumphed even over those who refuse, for God in Christ, Christ crucified, has the final word.

We should therefore determine to know nothing except Jesus Christ and Him crucified. This is not a gramophone record but a dye of rich and splendid colour which will never fade. We must bring every thought into captivity to Christ—the Christ of the cross.

6

THE RESURRECTION

JOHN WESLEY ONCE wrote to one of his preachers to tell him that he was reasoning when he ought to be praying. Now there is indeed a time for reasoning—and so a time for not reasoning. The apostle tells us to pray without ceasing. He does not mean the "long prayer" which kills a prayer meeting being lengthened to twenty-four hours in one day! He is warning against gaps in the life of prayer, intervals in which we lose touch with God. So we might advise ourselves: sometimes reason; sometimes refrain from reasoning; but always be in touch with God.

Once again there is a time and a place for apologetics, or Christianity defensively stated. St. Paul in prison felt that he was at his post to defend the gospel. Peter urged his readers to be always ready for defensive talk with the man who asks for a reasonable account of the Christian hope. But Paul was not always in prison and Peter and his readers were not always listening to requests. The characteristic work of both apostles was proclamation. They proclaimed because they knew. So it has been through the centuries. It is the mark of the authentic church that she *affirms*.

The church does not wait breathlessly for further proof. She knows already. Her life does not depend, in the last resort, on what the historian tells us, valuable though his researches undoubtedly are. Her life does not depend on the reasonings of the philosopher or apologist, though his work is certainly important. The life of the church is constituted by the Word of God and it is sustained by the Holy Spirit.

Apology, or in a more familiar word, defence, is directed towards the enemy who attacks the Christian faith or to the honest inquirer who criticizes. Both the enemy and the inquirer may be regarded as outsiders whom we seek to answer—and to win. But if there were no enemy and no inquirer the life of the church would still go on: your life is hid with Christ in God. And at the season of Easter the hidden life of the church bursts forth into joyous praise. On this day there comes into focus all that we have known throughout the Christian year. The Lord is risen indeed! On this day if on any day at all discussion ceases, books are closed, argument stilled. On this high festival the authentic church refuses to be bullied by natural law ("do miracles happen?"), enticed by the argumentative, beguiled by the doubter. The garments of mourning are shed and through our decorous worship there pulses a throbbing joy. In spirit if not in literal fact we are one with the Eastern Christian who shouts aloud that "Christ is risen!" and fires his gun exultantly against the wall of the church building.

What do we mean when we speak of "The Resurrection"? To judge by some people it is merely the religious recognition that spring has come again. The season of spring may serve as an illustration if the preacher needs one, but it is dangerous to use. It is limited in its scope, for it could only be properly used in the northern hemisphere. On the same principle a cynical speaker in Australia could argue that Easter is symbolized by the autumn or fall and that Christianity is a dying religion. More important is the fact that the illustration of spring could give the wrong impression of Christian truth. Spring comes every year and in "the liturgical year" Easter comes every year; but the Resurrection came once and once only. Our Lord Jesus Christ, for us men and our salvation, died once, and once only, once for all; and He dies no more. "Christ having been raised from the dead no longer dies; death has no longer any lordship over Him." And so there is no question of His being raised again. "The death which He died He died to sin once for all; the life which He keeps on living He lives to God." Christ is risen, once and for all. His resurrection was a single divine act: God raised Him from the dead.

Our Lord is thus not merely a Figure in a book or just a voice from the past. We gladly admit that He is recorded in a book, the Word of God written, and it is through that book that He is mediated to us by the Holy Spirit. Apart from the scriptures we should know little of the Son of God. But He is more than a character, even a historical character, in a book, like Julius Caesar or Alexander the Great. Caesar, being dead, dies no more; but he has not been raised from the dead!

One winter's evening in a large city in North America a friend of mine suddenly called her husband. "There's somebody on the next door roof!" Quickly he joined her at the window. Yes, it was true. Somebody was standing there.

The explanation is simple. Their own window looked out on to the roof of the building next door which sloped towards them. A floor higher up in their own apartment a man with a projector and coloured films was using the snow-covered roof as a screen. As he projected someone's picture on to the "screen" his neighbours below saw "somebody on the roof."

Now suppose the man had a coloured picture of a famous beauty; suppose that in the spirit of the artist he projected it on to the smooth snow night after night; and suppose that it became the talk of the apartment, the residents of which invited their friends from time to time to come and see the lady on the roof. It is not inconceivable that an innocent young man might gaze and gaze at the lady until he fell in love with her. How he longed for an introduction to her! But when his laughing friends explained the situation he would discover his folly. The rosebud of her lips was cold as the surrounding snow. She was a work of man's technique but had no life. Her beauty was entrancing but she had no heart. Radiant in colour she was but a picture.

Such is our Lord, if He is no more than the creation of the four evangelists, a Figure on the printed page. The wonder of His Person is no warmer than the cold print which describes Him. He is the creation of human art, but has no life. He may be the desire of all nations but, alas, He has no heart.

It is a big "if"! For—God raised Him from the dead. He is recorded in Holy Scripture indeed, for our learning; Scripture testifies to Him. But He Himself to Whom it testifies has mounted high and now sits, living, at the right hand of God.

Again we must ask what The Resurrection is and what it means. We must not think of it as only a spectacle, historical and awe-inspiring though it was. There is no appearance of the Risen Christ in the New Testament which is a mere appearance and no more. "Appearance" does not do justice to the evidence.

For instance, when I was once in London it was necessary to visit a friend who held office in one of the great railway companies. (It was the London office of a Canadian railway.) As I entered the large room with its long counter open to the public, I caught sight of my friend in the far corner. There he was in a private office of his own with walls of glass. It is a nice point as to whether he was "present"; he was hardly absent. He certainly appeared because I saw him. He did not speak. How could he? He did not yet know that I had arrived; and in any case he would not shout through glass walls across a large office. He appeared— that is all. It is not a picture of the Resurrection.

Again, we read occasionally of actors who will "appear" in this or that production. But we must not liken the Resurrection to an "appearance" on the stage in which our Lord monopolized the talk and the audience could not answer. The Lord appeared indeed to His own and He held personal communication with them. It was "this same Jesus," still bearing the marks of His wounds, Who renewed His former association with them. Fresh from His conquest of death He spoke to His disciples and they spoke to Him.

What then is this Resurrection to us who believe? And what are we meant to believe about it, if we learn from the New Testament? It is first of all a sign of the deity of Christ. There are signs indeed in the days of His flesh if the discerning faithful will but look deeply into the gospels. But this is the climactic proof. He had lived His life, faithful to His Father, obedient to the length of death. Was this the end, the wicked execution of a good Man? This seems to have been the thought which struck His former disciples. "We were hoping that He was the One Who was going to redeem Israel." But it was not the end. The last word was with God, Who raised Him from the dead and thereby showed Him precisely for what He essentially was and is, the Son of God. "Signalized in power as Son of God as a result of resurrection from the dead."

He is indeed human for ever more, as He has taken manhood into the Godhead. During His earthly ministry His disciples and all the world could see that He was human. In the synoptic gospels it stares us in the face as plain fact; in St. John's Gospel it is a fact and more than a fact: it is a dogma. Jesus is human. But it was the Word Which was made flesh. God's act in the Resurrection is the final proof that Christ is the divine Son of God.

That alters everything. It indicates and makes explicit that which was implicit in the earthly life and teaching, not least at the Last Supper, the Agony and the Dereliction. It is a sign that His death was not just another death in the sad story of men. It was an—it was *the*—atoning death. If the Lord were only a Man, even though a sinless and perfect Man, of what avail to us would His death be? Indeed it might be argued that it is unfair for an innocent Man to go to His death for sinners. Why pick on this Man?

But Christ is more than "an innocent Man." If, as the church teaches and the Bible proves, He is a member of the Holy Trinity, we may affirm with the New Testament that He shared in the work of creation. "All things were made by Him."

Then His responsibility for men in creation is extended to His responsibility for sinners in redemption. As Creator He was responsible for their existence; as Redeemer He voluntarily and lovingly shouldered the responsibility anew. He knew the verdict of the court was right; but He stood with sinners in the dock—or rather, He stood there alone, the Just for the unjust, that He might bring us to God. In the words of Sparrow Simpson's hymn, "Jesus is bearing it all in my stead." Only man can thus die; but only God can shoulder the responsibility. And He died, a sacrifice for sin.

God raised Him from the dead. It is a sign that the sacrifice has been accepted. Here we may see the mercy of God for our comfort. When Zacharias, the father of John the Baptist, lingered in the Temple, the people were waiting for him and because they knew nothing of his converse with the angel Gabriel they were wondering at his delay. The God of Israel was not to be taken for granted and they may have been anxious for Zacharias; in so sacred a place might he have incurred the divine displeasure?

Similarly men might wonder if the sacrifice of Calvary has been accepted. Without certainty here we are either still in our sins or else we do not know where we are. But Christ loved us and delivered Himself up for us as an offering and a sacrifice to God. Was Christ's sacrificial death acceptable to God? Did His death really atone? Yes! affirms the New Testament. Yes! preached the apostles. Yes! shouts the church universal in exultation. God raised Him from the dead. "He was delivered up because of our transgressions and raised with a view to our justification."

Once more, the Resurrection of our Lord is a sign of the future resurrection of the Christian. Now is Christ risen from the dead: what an anticlimax to our faith it would be, what a bathos, if at the end of our earthly life we came to an absolute end! But He does not remain alone in His glory. If in this life our hope is firm in Christ, and in this life only, then of all men we are to be pitied. We have built our all on a certainty, and it has crumbled into dust beneath our very feet. The firm foundation of God has become a quicksand. The rock has been disintegrated as by an earthquake. But now Christ has been raised from the dead and He stays "raised," the firstfruits of those who have fallen asleep in death.

It is an interesting metaphor which the apostle uses. The first-fruit is the first portion of the harvest. It is the first instalment, so to speak, of the harvest which is on the way. It tells the farmer that the seed has germinated, all the seed, but that this particular one is in advance of the rest. It is thus a pledge that the full harvest will come. The winter storms have not destroyed the crop.

It is like that with Christ. In—or after—His death He was sown as seed. He was sown in weakness and raised in power; He was sown in dishonour and raised in glory. When they die His people are likewise sown in their burial. But Christ is the firstfruit of the harvest. As He was raised, so they will be raised. Not yet have the sleeping dead appeared above the surface, but they will come up. The Lord's Resurrection is the pledge of theirs. If the Spirit of Him Who raised Jesus from the dead dwell in us, then He Who raised Christ Jesus from the dead will quicken (=make alive) our mortal bodies also through His Spirit Who dwells in us. He has already quickened them in one sense: the Spirit is life because of righteousness: the righteousness of Christians, pre-eminently imputed, then inspired and imparted and finally practised, is a sign of the life-giving Spirit of Christ within them. Christ Himself, the risen and living Christ, is within them by the Spirit. Will He fail to raise them later? Christ is the Firstborn from the dead, that He might be the first among all.

It is small wonder that the believing church, when true to her faith, does not dwell on secular intimations of immortality, least of all at Easter. She remembers that she is in Christ, Christ risen Who is alive for ever more.

There is challenge here, and comfort. Just as Christ was raised from the dead through the glory of the Father, so should Christians walk in newness of life. For the Resurrection of Christ was not only a metaphysical act of God; it is a moral claim on believing men. They are in Christ and in His Resurrection they were raised with Him, as we see pictured in baptism. They should therefore live a life to match their experience: they should live a "resurrection life." If you were raised with Christ, seek the things that are above, where Christ is in session at the right hand of God.

But were we raised with Christ? We were not there! But we were raised in principle. Just as in justification God treats us "as if" we had never sinned, so, when justified, we are "as if" we had been raised with Christ. How is this realized? The apostle tells his readers that they were raised with Christ through faith.

It is salutary therefore to ask ourselves if we put our trust in Christ, not nominally or formally but seriously and vigorously. Do we trust Him? Then we have indeed been raised with Him. Do we walk with a moral freshness? And in our walk are we "getting anywhere"? Do we "aim high"? That depends on our moral and spiritual seriousness. There is no easy mechanism in the life of the spirit. Discipleship is the working out in our lives of our faith in Christ and of our gratitude to Him to Whom we owe our all. He who is forgiven little, loves little. But should not we who have been forgiven much, love much? The quality of our life will be in proportion to the intensity and persistence of our faith. We make our own moral resurrection possible through faith—"raised with Him through faith"—and we stay "up" as faith is actualized through love.

When faith burns low the moral life becomes pedestrian. We know no soaring eagle's flight. But if our heart condemn us, God is greater than our heart and knows everything. Within that divine omniscience is God's knowledge of the Son, the risen Lord, Who is ever alive to intercede for us. By the Father's good pleasure the Son prays for His people, and He has the right to pray for them for He has redeemed them. If any man sin, we have an Advocate with the Father, Jesus Christ the righteous; and He is the propitiation for our sins. If we confess our sins God is faithful and righteous to forgive them—and righteous means just. Our Lord does not merely appeal to the Father's love; He addresses His justice. He Himself has paid the price and the Father is faithful to the cross and justly recognizes its finished work.

Here then is the comfort as well as the challenge. There is now no condemnation to those who are in Christ Jesus. Their own heart may condemn them but God does not, for they are in Christ. And through faith He has taken up permanent residence in their hearts.

All this we owe to the Resurrection. It is perhaps conceivable that without the Resurrection the Lord's atoning death might have been accepted by God and He might have continued His ministry in heaven of intercession for us. But without the Resurrection we should never have known and we should have continued to stumble through life, disappointed men and men without a certain hope.

But now is Christ risen! All this comprehensive truth will be in the heart of the church as she worships on Easter Day. It may be that in the northern hemisphere spring will gladden the morning. Grateful to God for His goodness, we shall yet not sound our deepest note of praise for the reminder of nature's recurring rhythm, for the inadequate symbolism of a returning season. Grateful to Him Who is Truth for every sound argument for immortality, we shall not find our peace in philosophic speculation. We shall rather dwell on Him Who suffered death upon the cross for our redemption; we shall meditate on that full, perfect and sufficient sacrifice, oblation and satisfaction for the

E

sins of the whole world; and we shall thank Almighty God for the glorious Resurrection of His Son Jesus Christ our Lord; for He is the very Paschal Lamb Which was offered for us, and has taken away the sin of the world; Who by His death has destroyed death, and by His rising to life has restored to us everlasting life.

We should notice the expression, "He has destroyed death." It sums up, negatively, what the Lord has done for His people. The cynic will criticize it for its unreality. Death destroyed indeed! Why, death is the foundation of morticians' fortunes.

The cynic is right when he points to the commercial value of death but he is wrong in his exegesis of scripture. It does not mean, and does not say, that death has been removed and that there is now no such experience as dying. That blessed time will be, but it is not yet. Then in what sense has death been "destroyed"?

During the World War II the people in England were at one time expecting to be invaded from the continent of Europe. Stringent regulations were made to prevent the civilian population from giving any help, however unwillingly, to parachute troops who might descend on them. In particular it was laid down that if any motorist parked his automobile and left it he must first remove the rotor. Without this little piece of mechanism the ignition would not work. No spark would pass across the plugs, no gasoline would be ignited and the engine would never run. The car was not destroyed; it was put out of action.

So it is with death. It still waits there, near or far, for each one of us; but, for the Christian, its deathliness has been taken away. Death, as death, has been put out of action. Its sting has gone, for the sting of death is sin; and believing men know that the Lamb of God has taken away the sin of the world. And they know because, as we have seen, the Lord is risen indeed. This will be their testimony on Easter Day. They will not argue but they will affirm; they will not speculate but they will be witnesses.

Whence do they derive their knowledge given in their testimony? They learn it from the evidence of Holy Scripture and by the inner witness of the Spirit in confirmation. That is why they are called to affirm. Those who are outside of Christ will never understand until they fall at the feet of Christ in repentance and faith. But:

> Nec lingua valet dicere
> Nec littera exprimere,
> Expertus potest credere
> Quid sit Jesum diligere.

Jesu, spes poenitentibus,
Quam pius es petentibus;
Quam bonus es quaerentibus;
Sed quid invenientibus—

The story is told of an explorer who took with him a carrier pigeon on his expedition. After long months in the Arctic snow he tied a short message to the bird which he then released. For long desolate miles it flew until at last it fluttered down into its home. The explorer's wife was sure, when the bird came, that all was well in the unknown. So when the Heavenly Dove came at Pentecost, the Holy Spirit, the apostles' remembrance of the Resurrection was vitalized and new converts were confirmed in their faith that Christ was alive. That same Spirit, by Whom Christ is present with and in His people, interprets Holy Writ still, and is the sign and seal that our Redeemer was raised from the dead and is alive for ever more.

7

THE HOLY SPIRIT

A GREAT SCHOLAR AND theologian, in the course of a serious illness, found himself wondering why the truths which he had preached to others now failed to bring him strength in his weakness. They still seemed true but the vitality had gone out of them. In his mind's eye he saw a great balloon, able to lift him high. But alas! he had not the strength to grasp its trailing rope. Later search and reflection show him what was missing in his life: he was neglecting the deep teaching of the New Testament about the Holy Spirit.

The modern church might well take this to heart. Is there a sickness with us? Are we strangely lacking in power? We are penetrating the suburbs of the great cities with our church extension; but is the message of the gospel entering the hearts of the suburban population? We build massive churches and chapels, to say nothing of cathedrals; have we a massive faith? We spend time and money on choirs and music; do our people know God? Our laymen give thousands of dollars for ecclesiastical bricks and mortar; will they give tens of thousands to the missionary cause? We institute a year of what we have termed intensified evangelism: a mission to the world; and what finally appears is a teaching mission to the church. Have our teaching missions the converting power of God? We have a vast programme of Christian Education and techniques in abundance; is it true that in many parts of the world Christian Education has threatened to become a substitute for the preaching of the gospel? We call ourselves part of the Holy Catholic Church (and we do not mean "Roman" but "universal"); is Hendrik Kraemer right in saying that everywhere the church is thoroughly secularized? If the Easter message of some is typical of all, then we are intellectually secularized and the church is very sick indeed.

Like the sick theologian we need to dwell on that article of the creed which we profess: "I believe in the Holy Ghost." But Who is He? (Notice that we do not say "What is It?" The Holy Spirit is not an It but a He.) The Holy Spirit is the Lord, just as much as our Lord Jesus Christ is Lord. He is the Life-giver, and so is the source of the vitality sorely needed by both theologian and church. He proceeds from the Father and the Son. Notice the phrase "and the Son" (*Filioque*). The Eastern and Western Churches divided on this issue and it is to the credit of the Western Church that she insisted on retaining the phrase.

What does it mean? If we leave it out and say that the Holy Spirit proceeds from the Father only, then it is pertinent to ask the question, "Who is the Father?" Show us the Father and it sufficeth us. But where can the Father be shown? "He that hath seen Me," said our Lord, "hath seen the Father." "No man cometh unto the Father except through Me." There is thus one way and only one way to the Father—through Jesus. That is why those who say that Jesus is a door, but not *the* door, are wrong, heretical and blasphemous.

The Father, then, is uniquely revealed in the Son. Are we to imagine that the Holy Spirit Who proceeds from the Father is free to depart from God's revelation in Christ? This could bring division between the Son and the Spirit. And can the Holy Spirit, as proceeding from the Father, reveal anything which is not already given in God's full revelation in His Son? There is a safeguard in the statement that the Holy Spirit proceeds from the Father and from the Son.

The Father sends the Holy Spirit in the Name of Christ. On the other hand the Son sends the Holy Spirit from the Father. The Spirit is the Spirit of God; He is also the Spirit of Christ, the Spirit of God's Son. He "reminds" the apostles of all that the Lord has told them. He quickens and vitalizes, and He glorifies Christ. He takes the things of Christ and applies them to men's hearts.

What does all this mean in our Christian experience? It means in effect the presence in our lives and hearts of the living Christ in power. Jesus Christ, the Son of God, risen, ascended and exalted, is present in our hearts and in the church generally only through the Spirit. In short, God the Father is unknown; but He is made known through Jesus, Whom by His grace we do know. The Holy Ghost has the character of Jesus and for practical purposes may be regarded as the presence of God in Christ in our hearts with power. Through Him, Jesus, we have an entrée, an introduction, in one Spirit to the Father. But this is the truth which we have forgotten or under-emphasized.

We need to remember it for our own soul's good; and we likewise need it for the work of the church. Without the Holy Spirit Jesus is inaccessible, and therefore with Jesus the Father is inaccessible also. Without the Holy Spirit the scriptures are not what they are with Him; without Him they are no more than cold print. Without the Holy Spirit prayer is at an end and the true fellowship of believing men disintegrates: they can come together with one accord to landscape the churchyard but not to explore the deep things of God.

And without the Spirit the outward thrust of the church will be a feeble speaking to ourselves. Consider the problem of "communication." The church has been criticized for verbalism, for an undue reliance on words both printed and spoken in communicating her message; for mere talk; and has been directed to search for new techniques. Hendrik Kraemer addressed himself to this same problem in his Laidlaw Lectures some years ago and Dr. F. W. Dillistone, former Dean of Liverpool, has approached it in his own way in his *Christianity and Communication*. Printing and radio, we are told, may go to the lumber room; the age of the printed book may be drawing to its close; the mass audience will look and listen.

It may be. But it is odd to reflect that such prophecies come at a time when the state, and especially the welfare state, is printing forms by the million.

This breakdown in communication is not confined to the church. It appears everywhere. Science is idolized and the attitude of many towards it is that of blind faith. In spite of the expansion of university teaching there are masses of men who are ignorant laymen when it comes to science. Specialization is so advanced that it is reported that sometimes in the same faculty scientists cannot communicate their ideas to their fellows. Science has its problem no less than the church, and art as well has its problem of communication.

Dr. Kraemer has his own suggestions to make. The church must purge itself of its secularism, of its tendency to identify itself with the culture of the age. As Dean Inge once said, if you marry the spirit of this age you will be a widow in the next. The church must go forth, like Abraham, not knowing whither it goes except that it is following the call of God. It must not *identify* itself with modern man and the modern mind but must *meet* modern man where he is. It must communicate *with* him before it can communicate the gospel message *to* him. The archetypal language of theology may be retained, provided it is interpreted. And the laity must be used far more than we have done in the

past. Perhaps it is with "meeting men" in mind that Dr. Dillistone
tells us that the missionary or minister must be deeply aware of
his own history, the history of those to whom he would minister,
and the history of Jesus Christ—my history, his history and the
Lord's history.

All these suggestions will be pondered. We have to do everything we can to make the message plain. But the fact remains that
Christian communication is in a class by itself. It is not only the
expounding of a doctrine, though it may include that; it is not
only the defending of a practice, though that, too, may be
involved. But first and foremost it is the conveying of a Person—
not the mere talking about a person but the actual giving of Him
to the receptive heart.

That alters everything. When we have tried every new device
and experimented with every new technical invention; and when
we have remembered that it is our task to discover the secret not
of successful communication but of faithful communication; then
we have to recall that in the last resort if our message is to be
received it will be only through the Holy Spirit. In the last
resort? That savours of the shipwrecked mariners in "The
Tempest": "All lost, to prayers; to prayers, all lost." No, not in
the last resort; as if we were to try all the techniques possible, and
find them failures, and then say, "I'm afraid we shall have to rely
on God." Such is an insult to the Holy Spirit and a sure explanation of our failure. We must start with reliance on the Holy
Spirit, knowing that nobody will be won to Christ unless his
heart is touched by this same Spirit. No man can say that Jesus is
Lord except in the power of the Holy Spirit. The Spirit is *Lord*.
And when the Word of God is preached, some He conquers,
interpreting the message and driving it home to their hearts; and
some in His sovereignty He does not conquer. "On whom He
wills He shows mercy and whom He wills He hardens." Have
we the confidence, the certainty, the faith, to face the world with
this message, knowing that it will be received by some; that it
will be rejected by others just as it was in the days of our Lord's
ministry ("there was a split among them"); and that it will be
received—and abandoned later—by yet others, just as our Lord
taught in the Parable of the Sower? "Will ye also go away?"

It is to be feared that the church is suffering from what Gilbert
Murray in another connection once characterized as "failure of
nerve": a weakness of lively faith; an uncertainty about our
message; a hesitation; even a lack of devotion. With some you
speak of theology and they answer you with philosophy; you

reveal your religion and they raise a problem of theology; you speak of the Lord Christ and they turn the subject to the church or to an argument, or have nothing but an unresponsive silence. Many of us have met the man whose ambition is to hear more about the church and less about Jesus Christ.

Now all this is profoundly disturbing. It is said that in the days of J. H. Jowett, the famous preacher of Birmingham, not a *month* passed without someone meeting him in the vestry in order to get right with God; that with Spurgeon there were conversions every *week*; but in the early church the Lord was adding *daily* those who were saved. Is it true that we do not expect this to happen today; that we do not want it? This seems to be the case, to judge by the way in which some people fight shy of any talk of conversion. And alas! they get what they expect.

We say that we believe in the Church *Militant*; we pray for a person "manfully to *fight* under Christ's banner against sin, the world and the devil, and to continue Christ's faithful *soldier* and servant unto his life's end"; we say that in Christ the forces of evil have been beaten and that it is now largely a question of mopping-up operations; we say that we believe in world conquest by the Kingdom of God. Why do we not enter with greater zest into local battles and skirmishes and victories? Why not rejoice at the capture of prisoners for Christ our Lord which we term conversion? Must we be like that German shell which started out to conquer but proved to be a blank and ended as the hot water bottle of a Belgian nun? Have we no certainty?

There was a certainty in the German Confessional Church under Hitler and the Nazis. An English ecclesiastic who visited Germany commented after his return on a German church service. He was greatly impressed by the "notices" which followed the creed. They were no formality as in some of our more comfortable traditions. They were the only source of church news, a sort of spoken parish magazine: the Rev. A.B. arrested, imprisoned or released or sent to a concentration camp; and the collection for his family. That is almost apostolic. And an announcement was made of a future meeting-place—with the Gestapo on their heels and but a day behind. Such a dogged continuation of the worship of God is not a characteristic of those who have lost their nerve; it is a sign of the presence of the Com*fort*er, the Holy Spirit Who makes a man *fortis* or brave.

Consider those church notices in the light not only of the dangerous situation but of the power of the Spirit whereby believing men continued in their faithful service and worship.

They raise some interesting questions. Can we so write and utter the announcements as the apostles themselves would have done? Can we so word them as they would appear if found in the New Testament? Not for the German Confessional Christians, not for the apostles, in the midst of worship, the urgent advertisement and request: "there will be a Wiener roast next Saturday; bring your own supplies and appetite"! What form would the notices take if written by an apostle or by an apostolic Christian of today? I suggest something like this:

There are three announcements:

1. We are all become unclean; but we all are not able to cleanse ourselves, nor to make one another clean. We are by nature the children of God's wrath.
2. But: whereas we were condemned to hell and death everlasting, God hath given His own natural Son . . . to be incarnated, and to take our mortal nature upon Him with the infirmities of the same, and in the same nature to suffer most shameful and painful death for our offences, to the intent to justify us and to restore us to life everlasting; so making us also His dear beloved children, brethren unto His only Son our Saviour Christ, and inheritors for ever with Him of His eternal Kingdom of Heaven.
3. Therefore: I propose to preach next Sunday morning, God helping me, to men who are still under God's wrath, and freely to offer them salvation in Christ Jesus. You who are already in Christ, bring with you those who are not, that they may hear the gospel of God's dear Son.

Some will criticize and say that this is simple, crude, unecclesiastical and fundamentalist. As a matter of fact the first two points were taken from the First Book of Homilies, which even today in the Church of England retain a measure of authority; and the second one was written by Cranmer. We can hardly bless Cranmer for his evangelical Prayer Book and revile him for his homily. We cannot accept his theology in the Prayer Book and repudiate it in the Homily. Admittedly the language can be modernized and the notices shortened. But the structure might well be retained. Such notices would show clearly that the church means business; that it is certain of its message; that it is determined to make it known. If they represented the overflow of the pastoral heart and were not merely a stunt by way of experiment they might well be a sign of the presence and power of the Holy Spirit.

It is the wonder of the Christian faith that the greatest minds find their deepest satisfaction in it—and the wayfaring man though a fool finds his life therein also. Every school of thought recognizes that one of the profound books of this century is *The Interpretation of the Fourth Gospel* by C. H. Dodd. And by an interesting coincidence, if you go into a simple cottage home in the country, where the Bible is read and reverenced and loved, you will find that it is St. John's Gospel which is soiled and torn with the honourable usage of piety.

So the gospel may be preached in its profundities, as St. Paul termed them ("the deep things of God"), to those who are already in Christ. But in communication to those outside of Christ we have to begin with its simplicities. Evidence, again from Germany, will aid us here. According to Baron von der Ropp, speaking in 1936, religion in Germany has been cursed by intellectualism. The common soldiers had never heard the gospel story in a simple and intelligible form. When they do, it appeals to many of them. This experience is not unknown here and now in England and in North America.

Those of us who try to lecture, teach or preach; who try to "communicate": carry a heavy responsibility. Who can discharge his duty? Nobody—unless we can say, and mean, that "I believe in the Holy Ghost, the Lord, the Life-giver." God is Sovereign in man's salvation and the Holy Spirit is Sovereign, is Lord, in men's conversion. No man will be converted and no man will be edified, apart from Him. What then should the church do in this matter of communication? Whatever techniques are used, whether still pictures or television, whether nativity plays or the full drama, there will have to be words unless we are to leave people in a fearful immaturity. We therefore suggest certain directions for every man who would communicate.

1. *Believe in the Holy Spirit.*

2. *Seek your message from God.* This does not mean sitting down and trying to make your mind a blank. Search the scriptures and pray for the illumination of the Holy Spirit in your study of them.

3. *Proclaim Christ with confidence.* You are not alone. God is working with you, giving you the message, interpreting it and driving it home into the hearts of the listeners whether in sermon, Sunday School lesson or private conversation.

4. *Expect things to happen.*

5. *Speak in the language of the people.* This is what the Holy Spirit has chosen to be done in the language of the New Testament—it is the non-literary, "common" Greek. If for local

reasons the language of the people is impossible, either because it would appear patronizing or because it might be offensive, choose illustrations from the life and language of the people. There is room for great ingenuity here. The author of the Fourth Gospel is sometimes said to use irony, whereby certain speakers unconsciously say something which has a deeper meaning for the readers. For instance, " it is expedient that one man should die for the people." That came from a Sadducee turned prophet without realizing it.

We ought to be able to take a leaf out of John's book. Cannot we recognize the "prophetic" when we see it? We have heard of the modern craze of "Rock and Roll". Could not some enterprising speaker put himself *en rapport* with his audience (if they are that way inclined!) by a brief reference to Rock and Roll and then ask what it is that characteristically rocks and rolls? It is an action appropriate to a ship in a storm. Let him develop this theme. They are rocking and rolling: do they realize that their ship is going to sink? All lives are shipwrecked apart from Christ.

Once more, we hear the song, "Oh what a beautiful morning, Oh what a beautiful day." Who made it? Who gave it? All things were made by Him—the *Logos*, the Word, Christ. The very sunshine that laps the unrepentant life makes it a debtor to Christ.

6. *Make plain the fork in the road.* When the Word of God is preached the road travelled by the listeners divides into left and right. Point it out. "I set before you this day life and death." It is here that the Holy Spirit brings His work in men's hearts to a climax.

Some people may not like this. A Committee on Evangelism (of all subjects!) reported at a meeting after a year's study that something different from "decision" revivalism was needed. . . . No salesman could operate with such restrictions. And the late Dr. Shoemaker was shocked to discover the proportion of church people who had never made a decisive Christian commitment but had oozed into church membership on a conventional basis, never dealt with spiritually or helped to a Christian decision.

There we see the two possibilities: no revivalism, nothing to revive, nothing to make alive, everything to keep the cold hand of sinful death upon men; or the Holy Spirit, the Life-giver at work to conquer men. You do not like "decision"? What do you really want people to be? Decided to be undecided, determined to be sloppy, adamant for drift? Or to settle this matter and obey the call of God and obey His gospel?

7. *Quote scripture to give authority to your words.* Some people may

mock, accusing you of merely hurling texts at innocent heads. Others will be pierced with the sword of the Spirit. A discerning historian, Professor H. H. Walsh of McGill, has written that if there is anguish in Canadian Christianity it consists of the loss of the Bible as a unitary and authoritative revelation. The anguish will continue until the scripture is recovered. In the meantime it should be remembered that God is pleased to own His own Word and to use it as His instrument for breaking the most crusted exteriors. The Holy Spirit is not a free lance; He is never separate from the Word.

8. *Repeat your message time and time again.* Obviously we must avoid the "gramophone record." But we can give variations, as musicians say, on a dominant theme. If you wish to put a proposal to the Russians, a diplomat tells us, you must have the patience to repeat it again and again, and the staying power to go on defending it until you can tire your adversary out, for only by so doing will you convince him that you really mean what you say and that he can take the risk of reporting to his government that he has failed to move you. Conversely, if you wish to move your Russian colleague from one of his positions, you must be prepared to hammer away at him till he gives up. The human heart is as hard to move as that of the Russian diplomat. Show, by repetition, that you mean what you say.

9. *Encourage the laity in their ministry.* The "laity" are the *laos*, the people of God, and they have an important task in making known the Word of God—and are in a position to do so. They have penetrated the enemy lines in office and store, in factory and club, on the highway, in the mines and on the lakes and oceans. They are daily at their post to do with wisdom and with courage precisely what our Lord wants done. The cartoonist, the late Sir David Low, once said that he was an agnostic, tolerant and inquiring of other views, open-minded, ready to be persuaded—but not by threats, promises, organ music, lofty architecture, magic words, intonations, vestments, ritual, massed choirs, or the company of vast crowds of people. What is there left to do? Nothing—except to witness. And that is the privilege as well as the duty of the layman. Let him tell his friends and acquaintances, as he takes and makes the opportunity, how many things the Lord has done for him.

In his encounter with unbelieving men the Christian man will undoubtedly hear criticisms and objections concerning church, Bible and the faith generally. Encourage him to bring such problems to the minister. If he has had a sound theological training he should know where to find the answers. Give them to the layman to take back to his workmates. If the question is sufficiently important, find a text which answers it and preach on it. And take every opportunity. Clergymen and laymen alike can speak the comfortable words of the gospel to sorrow and adversity, to loneliness and misunderstanding. Love is a universal language.

10. *Be direct and bold.* When you seek to "communicate" the message, address the congregation direct. Do not read an essay out loud, as if it did not matter whether the congregation were present or not. Set forth the truth of God without fear. If you are a clergyman, remember that you are a knight in armour ready for battle; not a carpet knight in an ecclesiastical beauty parlour. Let your ambition be to fight the good fight of faith in the pulpit rather than to bleat in the beauty of a building.

Fear not critics: every century has its libels and slanders. In Charles Simeon's day they engraved a church bell with the words "Glory to the church and damnation to enthusiasts." But Monsignor Ronald Knox's great book on *Enthusiasm* does not leave you with the impression of a rich and throbbing joy in the Lord. Today men would accuse the faithful preacher of being out of date or a religious isolationist on the ground that he bursts through the conventional bonds that would hold him in thrall from proclaiming Christ. Be a pastor; but do not spend the whole of the time in such a way that you coddle the one sheep safe and warm in the fold. Seize the ninety and nine and lead them to the great Shepherd of the sheep.

To sum up: let the Christian see his faith and work in the context of the whole people of God. Let the teacher and preacher likewise remember that though he may feel alone he is really a member of a team, the church of the living God, Whose Son is its Head, Whose victory is assured and Whose truth endureth unto all generations. In view of our previous observation that the Holy Spirit uses the Word and is never separate from it, we give the last clause in another translation. "He remains eternally loyal." The Holy Spirit is loyal to the Word of God written, loyal to the Word of God preached, and loyal to the preacher. This then should be the watchword of all preachers and Christian workers: I believe in the Holy Ghost; He remains eternally loyal.

8

CONVERSION

IT IS SOMETIMES said that our Lord became incarnate in order to tell us what God is like. This is true as far as it goes but it is not an adequate statement of the purpose of the incarnation. It limits God's revelation in Christ to what He *said* and it might be argued with some plausibility that much of His speech can be paralleled in the Old Testament. But he that hath *seen* Me hath seen the Father. Again, we are told that He came in order to tell us how to live, and once more it is true in part. There is a rich strain of moral and spiritual teaching in our Lord's words. But would information on how to live have produced the early church with its thrilling enjoyment of the gospel?

All such suggestions fail to face deeply enough the fact of sin. Of what avail is it to the sinner to be told that God is holy love? What benefit does he derive from learning a new ethic or from seeing it in actuality in Christ? And if we are further told that God is "like" a father and that He forgives sin, the pastor may find that the news is welcome to some but leaves problems for others. Will even a Father forgive *my* sin?

A principle is stated in one of the apostle's "faithful sayings." Sayings are not "faithful" like a well loved dog in a home. The statement which we have in mind is to be believed; it merits and should receive an unreserved welcome. It should not be limited or toned down in any way. "Christ Jesus came into the world to save sinners." The spell of Bethlehem lies on most Christians at Christmas time; but if we stop there the Babe has not grown up to complete His work. The grandeur of the Sermon on the Mount has caught the imagination of many, whether they confess to being disciples or not. But it needs to be read in the whole context of the New Testament if we are to see the gospel in it. He came to save sinners. Did He do it?

He cleared the ground. It is a confusion of thought to say that Christ "saved us on the first Good Friday." He redeemed us then, in common with the whole world. He made atonement for the sins of the whole world, and by His resurrection God showed that He had accepted the sacrifice. The Lord then let loose His preachers in the world with the gospel of His free grace. In virtue of His work they proclaimed repentance towards God and faith in our Lord Jesus Christ.

A sinner is not saved until he responds to God's invitation given to him in Christ. He has been redeemed; but salvation is not his until he has taken it. The gospel is made known to him through the Word of God written or preached; it may be taught in the Sunday School or in the home; but until a sinner puts his faith in Christ he belongs to the world which has been redeemed but not yet saved. Until that time (sometimes known only to God) in which he first believed, he has not yet tasted of salvation. "First faith" or conversion is thus of great importance as marking the beginning of the Christian life.

Having stated a principle, the principle of the incarnation, the apostle proceeds to exhibit an example. There may be men who think that conversion is not for them. Others may enter into the privileges and joys of salvation; but they themselves are beyond the pale. They are not good enough! Their sin and uncleanness would banish them from God's saving presence for ever.

To deal with such a situation Paul cites his own experience. Did Christ come to save sinners? Well, he himself is first and foremost in their company and he received mercy for a double purpose. God laid hold of him in sheer grace, to save him from himself, from the present evil world and from the fearful judgment to come. But there was a further purpose. In him first and foremost Jesus Christ demonstrated all His longsuffering.

This does not mean that the longsuffering is now exhausted; as if our Lord has put everything into the one case, all His mercy and grace and all His patience and willingness to wait; so that there is nothing left for other sinners. We must look at it in another way.

A few years ago there was a minor sensation when it was revealed in a motoring journal that on a deserted highway on a Sunday morning an automobile had reached the speed of one hundred and seventeen miles an hour. No prosecution followed because apparently there were no witnesses. But the deed had been done; the speed reached.

Now in recounting the event the driver could well tell his friends that his car "gave everything she had." He could vary the theme by saying that "she put everything into it" and by other similar expressions. It does not mean that having done it once the car could not do it again. It had been fully extended; it had demonstrated all its powers; in similar circumstances it could repeat the performance. It had demonstrated its full powers.

So we may understand "all the longsuffering" of our Lord in regard to the apostle Paul. How far will He go? How much will He endure? In my case, argues Paul, He went to the utmost. No sinner that ever was or will be needs any more longsuffering on the part of the Saviour than I received. He has demonstrated everything He has to give. He can do it again.

Here the sinner may be encouraged. He is not so bad that the mercy of God in Christ cannot reach him. He is not so God-less, idolatrous and selfish, that Christ gives him up, patience exhausted. He is not so evil that the Lord has no time for him. He had time for Paul; therefore He has time for you.

The conversion of Saul of Tarsus is accordingly of the nature of a test case. If he can be saved, anyone can. And Paul draws this inference. The demonstration of "all His longsuffering" was for the purpose of drawing an outline sketch of any and of all who would subsequently put their saving faith in Christ.

The word "cartoon" is not perhaps a happy one but it will serve. The skilled artist by a few strokes of his pencil is able to draw a figure of a politician or baseball player which is instantly recognized when it is seen. So by a few masterly strokes of the pencil we see drawn—converted man. Paul is not only an individual, though he is certainly that. He is a generic type. We called him just now "converted man" but it would have been strictly more accurate to speak of "man being converted." He is a typical case.

This runs counter to what many of us have been brought up to believe. When the discussion has turned to conversion and particularly to what is called "sudden" conversion, we have been warned off. We were forbidden to refer to Saul of Tarsus. "His is not a normal experience. His conversion was abnormal."

This is extremely odd, because it is the opposite of the apostle's own testimony. He regards himself in his individuality as the first sketch in a gallery of portraits of converted men, different no doubt in individual characteristics but still converted men. In his "typicality" he regards himself as the portrait of any converted man. He is not the abnormal. He is the normal. He is not the exceptional. He is the regular.

Now on the face of it this is odd, too. For when men are converted there is not the blinding light from heaven, brighter than the noonday sun. There is no voice which can be heard. There are no scales which fall from their eyes. In this sense indeed the conversion of Saul of Tarsus is exceptional. Today in conversion there is no light by which a photograph could be taken. There is no voice which could be recorded for posterity on a tape. There are no scales which could be picked up with a pair of laboratory tweezers. In literal matters such as these Paul is certainly the exception.

But the apostle is not thinking of this when he regards himself as the normal type. He means that if ever a man comes to Christ in conversion he follows a fixed pattern. It is true, as we gladly admit, that the wind bloweth where it listeth, and that such a wind is an apt illustration of those who are born of the Spirit. There are varieties of personality and in the manifold ("iridescent") wisdom of God the Holy Spirit may vary His approach or may appeal to this or that aspect of the man's character. He may appeal to his sense of gratitude or may speak to him when his life is in danger. He may threaten him with the law or woo him with the message of grace. But amid all such variation, and to be disentangled from it, is a consistent pattern. It is this pattern which we now seek to understand. If we can find it we shall begin to understand how St. Paul is the normal; his is a typical case of conversion.

To begin with, Paul is typical of the sinner *before* his conversion. It is sometimes said that when he was converted he did not turn from a false god to the true God. He was seeking to serve the God of Israel, the God of his fathers. But he was serving Him in the wrong way. Today the unconverted man may be serving a false god, whether it be the image of the heathen, the deified secular state or just himself in his selfishness. "Pride is idolatry." Or he may think he is serving the one, true God. But like the apostle he is serving Him wrongly.

His motive was wrong. He sought to earn his salvation. His works of righteousness—and many of them were genuine—were aimed at satisfying the divine requirements. We may suspect that he hoped to reach a certain standard which would give him a "credit" in the subject of life. The significant question of Paul the converted, "Where is boasting? It is excluded—the door is slammed on it," is a clue to his pre-Christian life. "Boasting" means taking the credit to yourself in gaining salvation, and that is what Saul of Tarsus was trying to do.

Closely allied to his wrong motive was his wrong method. He had a zeal which was not according to knowledge. His impetuous spirit turned seriousness into fanaticism. Though he had the scholar's knowledge of the Hebrew scriptures, he had not pene-

F

trated their deepest meaning and was largely a stranger to the idea of grace. Free grace was alien territory. So he completely misunderstood God. He was a legalist to the finger-tips.

On the earthly level he was not unsuccessful in his moral pursuit. There was undoubtedly a high moral rectitude in his life. He would not have indulged in any "shady" enterprise. He would have commanded a civic respect though it may be doubted if he would have inspired love. A certain stiffness and angularity, a certain rigid rightness, would give him a reputation for morality among men. He was a good citizen—and he knew it. By the standard of the righteousness involved in the law—"blameless."

This is his estimate of himself, and it was wrong. He thought he was standing on his own feet, and in theory he did serve the law of God; but when it came to the actuality of the flesh, of his unregenerate nature, he served the law of sin—as he recognized later. He had, proud Pharisee though he was, a relentless master whose demand always followed the same line. "The law of sin" is an expressive phrase. There was an imperative ever demanding obedience—the demand and the command of sin.

All these elements: wrong motive, wrong method, wrong estimate of himself, were fanned into a fanatic flame by his ardent zeal without knowledge, and it issued in a wrong character. It showed itself in the blasphemy of resisting the love of the Son of God; in the persecution of His people and the outrageous forms which it took.

Such factors as these vary in proportion in the uncoverted man. Not all such men are persecutors. Not all are zealous for righteousness. But there is a fatal flaw in their characters, created by their ignorance and unbelief. Their "ignorance" is culpable and their unbelief an affront to God. Every unconverted man is like the unconverted Saul of Tarsus in his lack of knowledge and faith. Even the many "high-minded" are outside the realm of salvation. Even John Wesley once said: "I went to America to convert the Indians; but, oh, who shall convert me?" It is small wonder that the Lord's long-suffering was fully extended and went "all out" in dealing with Saul. Some of the hardest to convert are the moral.

Objection is sometimes made to the statement that "good works" if done before justification are not pleasing to God. It may be answered in two ways. If they are done before being justified, then they are done in unbelief, because we are justified through faith. Such works are not pleasing to God as means to justification. In His love and mercy He has given us His beloved

Son, crucified for us. Is all that to be thrown away? If that be the
motive it must be unpleasant to God.

We may put this in another way—our second answer—by
means of an illustration. If a domestic servant reports to her
mistress that she has swept and dusted and polished all the bedrooms she may expect high praise for her energy and conscien-
tiousness. But suppose the mistress of the house makes reply like
this: "That is exactly what I did not want you to do. You have
spent all the time available on the bedrooms. But my friends are
coming to dinner tonight and I told you to clean the dining-room
and the drawing-room. You have greatly displeased me."
Nobody can assert that cleaning bedrooms is not "good"; but it
was not wanted at that time and it was disobedience. The
priorities were wrong.

So the earthly moral rectitude is "good." But it tries to put the
cart before the horse; it tries to be wiser than God; and it is not
what He asked for first. How can it please Him if done in unbelief? The sailor who neglects the work of navigation in order
to render excellent service in the restaurant will not please the
captain! All such mistakes arise from our forgetfulness that the
gospel is not only God's offer; it is His command. And all good
works done in unbelief are "disobeying the gospel."

Again, Saul of Tarsus is the typical convert *at* his conversion.
He was interrupted. He was intent on his own pursuits, seeking
his own righteousness, persecuting the church. Not every man is
morally serious before his conversion; and some are indifferent to
the church and to its Head rather than persecutors. But they go
about their own business. Then the crucified and risen Christ lays
hold of them—and interrupts them. It is in the interruption that
they follow the pattern of the apostle.

At the interruption there is an encounter between Christ and
the convert. With Paul there was no priest or preacher, no church
and no Bible—just the Saviour. "It is I, Jesus, Whom you are
persecuting." The experience was "pure," so to speak. With men
today it is mediated. The Word is preached; the testimony is
given; the Bible is read. But there is still the encounter. It may be
questioned if any man is converted without meeting with Christ.
But Christ does not address him from the heaven. He meets him
through the ministry of the Holy Spirit.

At such an encounter Saul passed from darkness to light. How
many people in the radiance of their conversion have been heard
to exclaim, "Now I see!" Some have even been known to declare
that their minister now preaches the gospel! What usually

happens, however, is that the convert is listening differently. He sees the meaning which before eluded him. He understands what is meant by such expressions as ". . . looking away unto Jesus. . . ." and ". . . we see Jesus. . . ."

Again, when Saul met with Christ and put his faith in Him, he passed from death to life. As he looked back he knew that in spite of all his legal blamelessness he had been dead in trespasses and sins; now he was alive in Christ. Then he had been receiving the wages of sin; now he enjoyed the free gift of God. Then he was dead while he lived; now he has eternal life in Christ Jesus our Lord.

This experience is repeated in all genuine conversion. The new Christian looks back on his past life and understands what the Damascus road meant to Paul, even though his own road to Damascus lacks the light and the voice. For he himself has repeated the pattern. He was dead and is now alive in Christ.

We have said that Saul—and any other convert—was interrupted. He received salvation, and it is important to notice that he received it from outside. This is not to say that Christian faith and life is not an inner, spiritual experience. It is certainly not a matter of external ceremonial or anything like that. There may be a measure of ceremony, like kneeling for prayer or walking deliberately to a lectern for the reading of the Word of God; but the outer act is nothing if the heart is wrong. Even so salvation is brought from outside; it does not rise up within. The impact of the living Christ means a revolution in the believer: a new release, a new programme and a new power. It is not an evolution of what is already present within. Salvation is brought from outside; it is within only when it has been received. It is not supplied by ourselves—otherwise we might as well identify sucking our thumbs with eating a square meal! Once again Saul of Tarsus and the convert of today speak the same language for they have received the same gift—from outside.

It was on the road to Damascus that Saul first put his faith in Christ, through which he received the grace of salvation. This is a most important thread in the pattern of the gospel. There are those who urge their fellows to love Christ, and no doubt it is true that a man cannot love Christ without believing in Him. But there is both grace and wisdom in the call of the gospel for faith. Could Saul the persecutor, even if his salvation depended on it, give his love to Christ? That surely came afterwards, when he had received mercy. So today to ask some hard-bitten men to love Christ is to ask the impossible: they cannot even love their own wives and children. But when their conscience is aroused they can throw themselves on His mercy; they can trust Him for forgiveness when in spiritual anguish they realize that they have no hope in earth or heaven apart from Him Who shed His blood for them. Later, with renewed mind and heart they can love Him for His unfathomable lovingkindness to sinful men. But at the time of their conversion their salvation depends utterly on faith.

Finally, Saul of Tarsus is the typical convert *after* his conversion. He was a puzzle to those who did not share his experience. On the Damascus road his companions stood speechless, for they heard him talking to Someone Whom they could not see. This is always a problem for the unbeliever. They may see a man on his knees and even hear his voice. But strictly speaking they cannot see him praying: they see the attitude of prayer, see a man in an attitude of prayer; but they do not really see "him-praying."

The Jews in the synagogues of Damascus were astounded at his immediate preaching of Jesus as the Son of God. They were confounded by his logic but unconvinced by his arguments. Festus, the Roman procurator, told him that he was mad—his mind unbalanced by his vast learning. Epicurean and Stoic philosophers in Athens, by contrast, regarded him as a man who had picked up bits of learning, much as a gutter-sparrow picks up mites of food here and there. Others thought he proclaimed foreign divinities contrary to the local tradition. At the Court of the Areopagus he was mocked by some and politely promised another hearing by others—the case adjourned *sine die*.

So it is to this very day. The testimony of a new convert in itself is a cause of astonishment. This man? Some vulgarly say that he has "got religion." They may admit the sincerity of his views and even the cogency of his arguments; and they cannot deny his testimony. But by no means all join him in his new faith. Some think him "crazy" in the abusive sense. Others see in his conversion the sad climax of his studiousness or on the other hand the mere retailing of unrelated doctrines which "he has picked up from the minister." Some take amiss his abandonment of the traditions of the club or of his circle of friends. The gentlemen promise to look into the matter with him—but not now; the ill-mannered merely mock. He remains a puzzle, and always will be a mystery to those outside.

There is a further parallel between this normal conversion and that of countless others. Saul's conversion was followed by prayer and he was baptized. On being received into the church he enjoyed Christian fellowship and immediately began his Christian service. For him it meant preaching Christ. With others it may involve any one of the multitudinous duties which come under the head of "church work," like teaching in the Sunday School or acting as an usher at public worship. It is all "doing something" for the Lord. His letters reveal the place he gave to baptism and to the Lord's Supper. He was a normal Christian and he followed the route which is characteristic of thousands. His leadership may have been abnormal; his missionary energy and strategy the activity of a spiritual genius; but in the general pattern he did what the ordinary convert does.

It almost goes without saying that he met with both opposition and welcome. There were those who would not stop at violence. The former persecutor became the persecuted. And there were those who heard the news as it was passed round that their quondam persecutor was now preaching as gospel the very faith which he once had been devastating, and "they glorified God in me."

The first and foremost of sinners has been converted. In common with all the world he had been redeemed by Christ. Now he has responded in faith. He has received Christ; he is in Christ. Salvation has been offered to him and he has taken it. His redemption was achieved on the cross. His salvation began when he first believed. The purpose of the incarnation has been fulfilled, for this sinner has been saved. And the offer is open to all.

9

FELLOWSHIP

A MAN RECEIVES SALVATION in Christ when he is converted. He should not be left to enjoy his new faith in isolation. We may wonder what happened to the Ethiopian eunuch after Philip had departed. He went on his way rejoicing. He may have encountered other Christians; or by his testimony he may have been the means of the conversion of others. Whatever took place in fact, it is not typical of the New Testament for a new Christian to remain apart from his fellows. Christian faith is personal and individual, but the believer's final resting place, even on earth, is not a pigeon-hole!

This raises the whole question of fellowship. It is a word which has become rounded and smoothed with usage, and much of its essential meaning has been lost. A learner-driver, for example, who has just passed his test as a competent driver of an automobile, may be told that he has now joined "the fellowship of the highway." Or a man may tell his wife one evening that he is going down to the church "for a bit of fellowship" when all he has in view is a game at the men's club on church premises. We are not criticizing but merely pointing out that the riches of the New Testament teaching and experience has been lost or at any rate by-passed.

Many of us have heard tales of old-fashioned steamers which puffed their way through the water with a great deal of fuss and very little progress. When some of them blew their whistle it was noticed that the thrust forward had slackened. Precious steam had been lost! There was not enough pressure for speed and noise. When the ship's whistle sounded it merely drew attention to itself. Advance had given way to mere noise.

So it is today with some sections of the church. We speak much of fellowship but what we produce is little more than noise. We emphasize our church activities and they just draw attention to themselves—with no advance, no conversions, no real fellowship.

But what is fellowship, according to the New Testament? Its

study is somewhat elusive, if only because of the limits of grammar, as great scholars like J. H. Moulton and F. Blass have shown. Some questions have to be dealt with by exegesis rather than grammar, though even here the exact meaning may escape the most skilful exegete and a theological interpretation must be brought in. But the search is a fascinating one, and the doors left open by grammar and exegesis give ample scope not only for linguistic ingenuity and theological sensitiveness but also for the guidance of the Holy Spirit.

The chief characteristic of fellowship, and one which gives us a sound clue for penetrating its mysteries, is that there is always something *"common"* to those who are authentic members of the Christian *comm*unity. Our point of departure is the frequently quoted text in Acts 2: 44 (see also 4: 32), "they had all things common." In this context "common" means "shared and shared out."

There are not lacking people who speak of a primitive Christian communism. What we see in the early church, however, is very different from the communism before our eyes today. It was in the church, not in the world. It was spontaneous and rose up from within; it was not a legal requirement imposed by an act of a Parliament or Congress from without. It was inspired by love, not by an ideology. It was a particular case, not a universal Christian practice. It was natural, not the result of a revolution. It was open, not brought about by the work of fifth columnists or fellow-travellers. It was not concerned with the proletariat as such and was not class-conscious; it had no political programme and knew little if anything about organized production.

This quantitative sharing and sharing out is the lowest form of Christian fellowship. If the church had persisted in it, the whole scheme would have become impossibly unwieldy, and it might well have become a hindrance to evangelism. If everything had to be shared out, supplies would have run short as more and more people entered the church, especially if many came in search of the loaves and fishes. If potential new members had possessions they would soon have learnt that they would be asked to put everything into the common pool, and the church's proclamation that it was offering a gift to the world would have been stultified.

We must make no mistake about this. The fellowship of believers has something to give to the world, and churches today have found to their cost that that truth is likely to be forgotten when the strangers within our gates are constantly met with appeals for money. It is unhealthy when outsiders get the impression that their bank balance must be inspected as a condition of membership.

We cannot escape this dilemma. If everything is quantitatively shared out, either the greater the membership the smaller the share; or the new member must surrender his possessions. In the former case the scheme will sooner or later lose its point; in the latter the new member must virtually purchase his membership and in time—if not from the beginning—will believe in justification by works or by cash.

But "common" means also "shared and not shared out." We read of the "common faith" and the "common salvation." This is a qualitative, not a quantitative, meaning and it is at the heart of the New Testament conception of fellowship.

How then shall we describe fellowship? There is a picture of it in the business activity of James and John, the sons of Zebedee. They jointly owned a little fishing fleet. With its equipment and sundry other articles it constituted the capital of their business. If they were joint owners it is correct to say that the fleet was "common" to them. James and John and Simon Peter were the partners in the fishing business. Instead of calling them partners we shall follow the Greek and call them "commoners." Their business partnership was then a "community." The partners were members of a little community; they were the "commoners" in the "common" fleet.

This is a simple illustration of Christian community, which is what is meant when we speak of Christian fellowship. It is best to keep the root *comm-* because it shows us the link: the commoners have a common interest in that which is common to them, and the whole set-up may be called a community. We may speak of fellows in the fellowship but we cannot say that the fleet is "fellow" to them: it is common to them.

Now Christian community (or fellowship) has its static and its dynamic side. With those who are in Christ Jesus it is not a question of a commonly owned fleet or of any material possessions. We have a common salvation. Each commoner in the Christian community has, in principle, the whole of the common salvation. Our share does not diminish every time a new convert is made! Each has all. Suppose, then, that there is a believing man in Sydney, Australia; and that there is another such man in London or New York. As men of faith they are justified; they have salvation. In other words, salvation is common to them. But they may never meet on earth; may never correspond by letter; may never even know of each other's existence. But they have none the less a common salvation. They are therefore related to each other in the Christian community. They are "commoners" in the common salvation. Their relationship to each other is static. This is indeed the fellowship or community of relationship.

But suppose, on the other hand, that a crowd of such men gather together for worship; for the preaching of the Word of God. The New Testament speaks of men gathering together "with one accord." They may meet in the Temple; they may meet in a private house. The scene may change from day to day. But they come together to some central rallying-point (*epi to auto*) which is ultimately spiritual rather than physical. They come to meet the central Christ, Who is common to them. The fellowship of relationship continues but now there is an added factor: there is the fellowship of experience. They are commoners— together; they are the commoners of the community—together. Salvation is common to them—and enjoyed together. This is the thought behind the vague use nowadays of the word "togetherness." There can be a secular "togetherness" in, say, a crowd watching a football or a baseball match. The Christian "togetherness" is the fellowship of experience—in Christ.

This understanding of fellowship or community is a key to unlock many doors of interpretation. Only grasp the significance of common, commoner and community and we shall see the richness of New Testament fellowship. In our Lord's words about the vine and the branches, for example, we can detect the common life flowing through the "commoners"—the branches—in the Christian community, which is vine and branches together. If we think of the Good Shepherd we are led to the common Shepherd, the "commoners" who are the sheep and the community which is the flock. If we speak of the Christian brotherhood we mean that there is a Father Who is common to the commoners (the brethren) in the community which is the brotherhood. We should look for this pattern whenever we see such words as communion or fellowship in the New Testament; and then we should see if the same pattern is to be found in the various metaphors.

We shall not now keep on speaking of common, commoners and community but dwell on community alone, bearing in mind that the other two terms are latent. Fellowship or community may be described as a purposive association as a means to a common goal. We do not mean to imply by this that the church, the Christian community, was founded by a number of people coming together like a committee and constituting themselves a church.

We mean rather that Christians do not just drift together unconsciously and listlessly stay together. A believing man *believes*
and it is *he* who believes. It is not an accident like slipping on a
hidden piece of ice. However he was originally drawn to the faith
he now deliberately believes. And he finds other like men in his
new Christian fellowship.

Visitors to Southern Ireland used to find walls and buildings
plastered with the words: "Two million Irishmen can't be
wrong." It suggests the strong convictions of the two million and
the common purpose which unites them. The purpose which is
common to the members of the New Testament association is of
still higher importance and it is instructive to notice the common
goal.

Sometimes the "common goal" is Christ. Paul speaks of being
called into the fellowship or community of God's Son, Jesus
Christ our Lord. What is the "common" element here? If we
translate fellowship or community by the word "participation"
we see that we are called to share in Christ: He is common to
those who have responded to the call. Elsewhere it is the Holy
Spirit Who is "common"; or the Body and Blood of Christ. On
occasion the common goal may be expressed in abstract terms, as
when the apostle speaks of Christian service, or spreading the
gospel, or suffering ("the fellowship of His sufferings"). We may
put it in another way. The people of God are one in their purpose,
their common goal, to know Christ, to receive Him afresh into
their hearts, to realize His presence, to spread His glorious Name
abroad, to serve Him, to "sympathize" with Him and to suffer for
Him.

The emphasis must now shift to the commoners. Christian
fellowship or community is the participation of different kinds of
means towards the attainment of a common goal. Imagine a
soccer team composed of eleven goalkeepers! Or a baseball team
every member of which was a marvellous pitcher but hardly knew
one end of a bat from the other! For the common purpose of
winning the game there must be different kinds of people in the
one team: someone to pitch and someone to bat and so on. It is
not otherwise in the Christian community. The people of God is
the most assorted, variegated, heterogeneous community on
the face of the earth, made one in the common purpose of the
Kingdom of God. Hence we read in the King James Version that
"there are diversities of gifts, but the same Spirit." There are
different kinds of talent, different kinds of service, different kinds
of result. One man is wise; another has knowledge; a third is a

brilliant example of faith. Yet another has healing gifts or an insight into the meaning of current history and politics. We are thus not "birds of a feather" flocking together. That is an everyday occurrence. The Christian community is something far more miraculous. Here the royal eagle flies happily with the grubby city sparrow; the social lion lies down with the humble lamb. Here, as in the early days, free Perpetua and Felicitas the slave face the hostile world together.

Each makes his own peculiar contribution towards realizing the common goal. Hence, as Paul exhorts, one man shows the relevance of the Christian faith to the times; another concentrates his gifts into channels of Christian service; another is a teacher; another is a stimulus to the church, indulging in what Mr. Wendell Wilkie called "public prodding," though, as befits a Christian, with the prickles removed. Another calls the needy to share his home or his food; a leader takes swift and conscientious thought for the duties of prominence, and he whose heart has been touched knows how to show pity without a long face. And all show love without humbug, because all are one in Christ, in the Holy Spirit, in faith, in spreading the gospel, and perhaps also in suffering and even in the divine nature itself.

One of the happiest examples is addressed by Paul to the church at Philippi. "No church had fellowship with me in an account of giving and receiving except you alone." It is a commercial metaphor. No church had fellowship with him in a credit and debit account. The immediate term which is common, which expresses the purpose in which the apostle and the church shared, is the general "financial dealings." He received; they gave. It was certainly the participation of different kinds of means in the attainment of a common goal.

Tennyson has illustrated this principle in Christian fellowship.

> Not like to like but like in difference,
> Yet in the long years liker must they grow;
> The man be more of woman, she of man;
> He gain in sweetness and in moral height,
> Nor lose the wrestling thews that throw the world;
> She mental breadth, nor fail in childward care,
> Nor lose the childlike in the larger mind;
> Till at last she set herself to man
> Like perfect music unto noble words.

Where "two or three are gathered together in My Name," there we may look for perfect music set to noble words.

All this is implied by St. Paul in his figure of the body and its members. There is one body and there are many members, each contributing its own gift to the common life. The eye cannot look down on the nose because it cannot see. The nose cannot turn itself up in disdain because the eye cannot smell. It takes all sorts to make a body, a world, and the Christian community. Let each member play his part, great or small, prominent or obscure, teaching or taught, uttering the prayers or saying amen to another. Therefore, be it understood: be yourself; your redeemed self. And do the task which is specifically yours. "I planted; Apollos watered; God gave the increase."

Such a Christian fellowship abides. For it is an association of persons bound together by some common element, not created by them or by luck, but accepted by them. The writer of the Epistle to the Hebrews refers to the fellowship of flesh and blood. It is the fellowship of the human race and is on the natural plane. No human being can contract out of it. A man may despise or hate his fellows, for they are still his fellows; or he may live the life of a hermit and avoid them; but he still shares with them a common humanity. The human fellowship is accepted by him because he can do no other. In his heart he may reject it but in actual fact he has to endure it. Nothing can alter the fact that he is a human being and that his fellows are human beings also. They share, even against his will, a common humanity. By definition *he* belongs to *them*. They are human and he is human. "A man's a man for all that"—even if the man happens to be himself.

Now this is but an illustration, but the same thought seems to have struck the apostle Paul with regard to the Christian fellowship. "The bread which we break, is it not participation in the Body of Christ? seeing that there is one loaf, we, the many, are one body." Why is this? "*For* we all partake of the one loaf." The communion service sets the seal on membership of the fellowship. We believers who partake, belong. We cannot escape that fellowship. We cannot contract out. Because we partake, therefore we are one body.

A man for reasons of his own may stay away from the Lord's Table and from the services of worship; he may even ask for his name to be removed from the church roll. He is denying himself the dynamic fellowship of experience; but if his faith is authentic he still has the fellowship of relationship. The salvation which he still enjoys in Christ is not his private possession; it is still the common salvation.

"The fellowship from which there is no escape" is an aspect of the fellowship to which the saved belong. This carries with it the further implication that each different and peculiar person who belongs to the Christian fellowship really does belong. If we fall into the temptation of denying or envying the other fellow, he is still a fellow in the fellowship of the people of God; still a commoner in the Christian community. And if the position is reversed and we ourselves are unhappily envied, despised or even insulted, the comforting truth remains—and the challenge also—that we still belong to the fellowship: they who offend against us are likewise still within the fellowship, members of Christ, heirs of God and joint-heirs with Christ. They and we alike have a common Saviour and in spite of ourselves we belong to each other.

In all the differences among Christian men, whether it be at the level of the local church or parish or in those large theological disputes which divide men, we ought at least to bear in mind the possibility that the other side may still "belong." There is a point of separation, admittedly. "They went out from us but they were not of us." But we should be very sure before we refuse fellowship. We might be rejecting those who really belonged to us in the fellowship of relationship; for Christ has continued to receive them.

Such, then, in outline is Christian fellowship. It embodies a common purpose, a diverse membership and mutual tolerance, with the living Christ flowing through each member as the common life of all.

Where is such a fellowship to be found? The obvious answer is that it may be found where the Lord left it—in the world. That is true, and we shall come to that point in a moment. But first we should notice that it is not only in this world of space and time. There is but one Christian fellowship and its membership is ever increasing. When a Christian dies his name may be taken off the church roll of the parish. We cannot have the parish of St. Paul's or St. John's with five thousand "dead" members and five hundred "living." We must use our commonsense. But those who are dead to us are alive unto God and they still belong to the Christian fellowship.

In a striking passage in the Epistle to the Hebrews we are told that "you have come to Zion, mountain and city of the living God, to the heavenly Jerusalem and to myriads of angels, to the festal assembly and church of the firstborn . . . and to the spirits of just men made perfect. . . ." "You have come" is a perfect tense and it implies that "you are now there." In a very real sense, and especially when we pray, the church on earth is in heaven with its multitude of angels—and church members. We dwell on earth, but "your life is hid with Christ in God." There is a commerce between heaven and earth.

Here we must be careful not to suggest anything in the nature of spiritualism. "The communion of saints" does not mean the communication of saints. God has not given to His people the means of communicating with one another from earth to heaven and from heaven to earth. But they are still members of the one fellowship and they still possess the common salvation.

It may be helpful to illustrate this. I was once away from home for a weekend preaching engagement and during some spare time turned on the radio for a news bulletin. The thought came to me that my wife was listening to the same broadcast and somehow it seemed to bring her near. We had the programme in common. So the people of God on earth listen to the same "programme" as their fellows in heaven. Each groups listens to "this same Jesus" as He speaks to them.

Or put it in another way. Let us suppose that a pilot of an air line regularly flies across the Atlantic. His wife is in America. Her parents are in England. She is concerned for them as she rarely sees them. But the pilot goes to see them every time he is in England. He tells them how their daughter is faring in America. On his return he gives his wife the latest news about them. Are they old? in failing health? perhaps in need? "I've fixed them up."

Now the pilot is "common" both to his wife and to her parents. Wife and parents do not meet but he is the link between them. They may not communicate but they do "commune." He looks after them ("I've fixed them up") and he looks after his wife also. So the fellowship on earth is tended by the Good Shepherd; and the fellowship in heaven is likewise in His hands. Members on earth and members in heaven may not meet and may not communicate; but they have Jesus in common, the Saviour Who keeps both church militant and church triumphant.

Jesus, the Mediator between God and man, is thus also the Mediator between Christian and Christian, because He is common to both. But we must now look at the fellowship where we mainly see it: on earth. It is certainly "in the world."

We may be urged to "come ye apart and be ye separate" and we do not misunderstand or lack sympathy. But whether we like it or not the Christian fellowship is *in* the world though it is not *of* the world. There are, alas, worldly Christians, but we are now dealing with principles rather than aberrations. To some extent the whole membership is in the world. Does a Christian own property in any form? Does he own his house? Has he some savings? Or has the church or a society within the church some investments or some buildings? The secular state comes in. There are laws concerning securities and there are laws concerning safety regulations for buildings. In a time of dearth Christians buy food ("rations") determined by the state. In some countries they travel on state-owned railways or air lines. Many are called into the armed forces. Lawyers are often required to defend evil-doers. We are indeed *in* the world. What then is the function of the Christian fellowship in the world? What is its task?

It is called to witness, and to witness unceasingly. We are to be a persistent evidence in and to the world. As Pericles said in a famous funeral oration, "We have a constitution which is not a rival of the institutions of neighbouring states; on the contrary we are an example for anyone rather than imitators of others." That describes our duty. Ideally, however much we may fall short, and whatever the world may think, the Christian fellowship is not just one of a number of rival bodies, a sociological entity among other sociological entities, trying to impress the world with our importance. We may appear to be a sociological group; some churches may even culpably give that impression; but strictly speaking the church in its fullness is more than that and is above a vulgar rivalry with other groups—even though called to war on all evil. The Christian fellowship is an example, is evidence, and it lasts, for the comfort of its friends and the confusion of its foes.

It may be overwhelmed by the tide of the world at some point in history. But the tide will go down. On a lovely little beach in the south of England there is a fresh-water spring which bubbles up an unfailing supply of pure delight. Twice a day the tide of the sea comes up and passes it; and twice a day the tide goes down and leaves it, not exactly high and dry but high and still flowing. The Christian fellowship may be covered and apparently lost as the world's waves come swirling over it; but the tide goes down and there are still believing people enjoying the common salvation.

St. Paul tells us that "if our gospel is hidden, it is hidden among (not "to") those who are perishing." What an opportunity for the world! There it is: in their midst. Are there infidels and agnostics in Parliament or Congress? But there is a gospel hidden there also. I think I hear some "commoners" of the Christian community offering a prayer. Is there a secular element in the teaching profession? Yet there are Christian societies as evidence of a non-secular power. Is there unsanctified merriment in a tavern? There

may also be a radio, to awaken by means of church bells the
memories of an earlier day. Was there swearing on a crowded
street car? But I see a text there, put up by an evangelistic agency.
At any time, in any place, except in the few, if any, God-forsaken
places, the veil may be removed among those who are perishing
and they may see the glory of God that was hidden among them.

Britain and Europe, whatever the character or indifference of
the inhabitants today, are steeped in Christianity and bear the
vestigial marks of many centuries. To a large extent the present is
the product of a Christian past. The impact of Christ on the
world has left its marks in the buildings, the culture and even the
language of today. Mr. Khrushchev can refer to a Judas or to
thirty pieces of silver. In America the long history of Europe has
been telescoped and in many ways the "newness" of the New
World is different from the Old. But still there are the traces of
the impact of Christ. Our gospel is hidden among those who are
perishing. We hardly need to take it to them, but to uncover it.
There is the evidence; there is the example, in stone and street and
speech. It is for the fellows of the Christian fellowship to live the
evidence in their warm flesh and blood.

Of what, it may be asked, is the Christian community to be the
persistent evidence? The short answer is, in the words of our
Lord, that "ye shall be My witnesses"—His witnesses about Him.
This may be broken down into various aspects of our witness.
The Christian fellowship should be a solid block of evidence,
which will not disintegrate under criticism or attack, of the
reality of the invisible. Throughout the land are thousands who
belong to Christ: visionaries and idealists, a sprinkling of poets,
hardheaded (but not hardhearted) business men in crowds, and a
rank and file almost without number who have known the
insistent claims of the material world by their own desperate
need; and all of them united in this, that they know the living
God, have found that He satisfies their deepest longings, inspires
their choicest acts of self-denial, stimulates their most imaginative
plans for the welfare of others, and saves them from their sins. In
a drab environment they are men who gaze upon the gorgeous
palaces of heaven; where men are dying, they enjoy eternal life;
when man's hand is turned against man and all are groping for
some inner certainty, they themselves in Christ are constantly in
the presence of God. To the seeking, blundering world the very
existence of the Christian community shouts aloud: "Whom ye
ignorantly worship, Him declare I unto you." And the Christian
preacher, the focus and the spearhead of all the "commoners" in

G

Christ, gathers up their collective evidence as he preaches the Word of God. The Desire of all nations has come.

The things which are seen are temporal; but the things which are not seen are eternal. And the unseen reality to which we bear witness among men who live by sight is the source of all comfort. This is not weakness, or a sentimental appeal to a shallow age. Has the strong man never watched over his fevered child, stood by an open grave or felt frustration in business? Has he never known the awful experience of disillusionment when he has found that his erstwhile idols have clay feet? Has he never been betrayed? Is he never a patient, needing the care and love of friends?

It has been said that in the ancient buildings of the Christian heritage, where men have worshipped God in Christ for centuries, we find an ancient house of mystery to refresh our spirit; a peace which stills the turmoil of the world; a new vision of the backgrounds of life which will lend perspective to our earthly problems. It may be so. To sit still in an old church on a weekday and be steeped in the atmosphere of devotion may bring back a steady look to our eyes and a more even rhythm to our pulse. Under its benign influence our normal scenery may lose something of its desolation.

It may be so. God uses the material to remind us of the spiritual. But it is in the Christian society itself where burdens are shared, man stands by man in trouble and sorrows are healed. For this is not a secular friendly society but a community of believing men in whom Christ dwells. He is the common Saviour, and the robust faith in Him shared by the community strengthens the faith of the broken-hearted. Leaning on the Christian fellowship a stricken brother learns afresh that in the Christ he serves is newness of life, vision, hope, sanity and strength.

The Christian community is thus the scene of our Lord's continuing ministry. Each member is a witness—and evidence—to the others, and the whole fellowship is an ever open door of benediction to the world. For the world sees. Encouragement sometimes comes from unexpected quarters. At the close of the 1914-18 war a huge meeting was held in London to celebrate the peace. The vast congregation sang "O God, our help in ages past." On the platform was George Bernard Shaw and at the end of the hymn, with deep emotion, he whispered to a man whom I later met: "I would rather have written that hymn than all my foolish plays." The same man told me a story about Keir Hardie, the labour leader. Asked if he would follow the same course if he had his life all over again, Keir Hardie replied: "No, Doctor, I would enter the pulpit."

The appeal of a hymn! The appeal of the pulpit! That is the impact which may be made by the Christian fellowship. Such is the grace of the fellowship of those who gather round our God, our help—our common salvation, common to all the commoners of the Christian community.

We hear much today of the appeal which atheistic communism has to the underdog, who is reputed to have nothing to lose but his chains. Certainly poverty is a fertile field for propaganda; hungry men will try anything once and are easily duped; and the lowest income brackets cannot fail to be attracted by the idea of a classless society, where they will have their place. But we shall never have a really classless society, though the form, the framework, of the classes may vary.

For look at the facts. Is it likely that the son of a dictator has no privilege? Has the wife of an important party official no advantage? Is a socialist cabinet minister of no more importance than his office boy? Is a left-wing Professor of Economics on the same level as a commissionaire? Knowledge of the facts—and of human nature—can give only one answer.

Now it is the glory of the Christian fellowship to be able to face this problem of the differences among men. It is its genius, not to clip the wings of its eagles and dress up its snails in fine feathers, reducing both parties to a dull pedestrian partnership in the new bravery of a suburb, all in the interests of an egalitarian cliché; but rather to take the high and the mighty on the one hand, and the humble and weak on the other, and bring them together to the foot of the cross and to the Lord's table. The General may come in civilian dress and the sergeant in uniform; but nothing will alter the fact that the one is a General and the other is not. But they come to the same Table, sharing a common Lord. It is not quite true to say that the distinctions have been obliterated. They have been transcended. The General is still a General and the sergeant is still a sergeant, but these distinctions, though still in force, *do not count as qualifications for coming*. To each man the Lord has said: "Come unto Me. . . ." and each has responded by coming to a common Saviour.

This is the problem which the church has always had; and this is the miracle which has been performed: and this is the solution of the problem of "class"—and the example and evidence which we have to set before the world. We sometimes say: "Let this mind be in you which was also in Christ Jesus." We might also say: "Have the mind in company which you have upon your knees." If each commoner has that, then the Christian community is evidence to the world, a working model of the Kingdom of God.

In that Kingdom God rules in Christ. The Christian fellowship is therefore a persistent evidence of the supremacy of Christ. Not everybody has consciously and joyously come under His rule. The humanist looks at man and says what a fine fellow he is. The scientist—or many scientists—looks at man's reputed origin and speaks of an animal ancestry. The Christian community looks at the possibilities in Christ, and says how profoundly saved man can be by His merits and power. Our Lord is supreme in man's salvation and His supremacy is reflected in all the thinking of His commoners.

The writer to the Hebrews took pains to prove that Christ is superior to angels, as a means to showing a yet greater superiority. His method is very suggestive. In those days the angels were regarded as being in possession, as it were. They ran the universe. The writer therefore takes what is highest in men's thought and affirms, and proves, that Christ is higher.

Today the picture has changed. Modern men do not in fact set much store on angels. They think rather of natural law and the achievements of science. "There is positively nothing that science cannot do," asserted a dogmatic and atheistic doctor some years ago. Learning from the Hebrews the Christian community looks at this "highest" and triumphantly affirms that Christ is higher. He is superior to natural law and to science. He invented natural law and He created the scientists. Christ is enthroned in nature, in history and in grace. He is Creator, Ruler and Saviour. The Christian community, with a lighter touch, is a witness to all the devotees of the modern religion—the idolatry of games. The hand that holds the stars in their places makes ball games possible. The fans would look rather ridiculous if after a mighty hit the ball sailed off into space and never returned! The first such hit might be claimed as a home run, but suppose every ball was thus lost? It is Christ to Whom the spectators are ultimately indebted for their game and for their enjoyment.

Such, then, is the first task of the Christian fellowship: to be an example to challenge the world to a like faith; to be a piece of evidence of God's saving goodness and grace in Christ which cannot be destroyed.

A further task is to be the living conscience of society. If the price of liberty is eternal vigilance, then governments in power

and social influences and trends need to be watched. The Dean of
King's said in the early thirties that "the power of the modern
state is colossal." What would be his thoughts today when there
is a mass of complicated legislation to add to the existing burden?
Now states, no less than individuals, are under moral obligation;
governments, as well as subjects, have their moral duties. God
has His rights as much as citizens, even in a democratic society.
We have got rid of the divine right of kings. There is no divine
right of democracies. The "mandate of the people" is not free
from moral obligation. Political expediency, especially when
flushed with party triumph, has still to recognize and obey the
moral law. There comes a point when a matter which at first
seems purely technical becomes moral, quite apart from the fact
that it is a moral imperative to be politically intelligent.

Social trends gather their strength and are often defended by
reference to the freedom of the individual. But we are not given
our freedom in order to abuse it.

In the contemporary situation the Christian fellowship is a sort
of gigantic crystal, resembling on a vast scale the original crystal
(with its "cat's whisker") used in the old radio sets. The community is the crystal; each commoner is—or ought to be—a "live
spot" of sensitive conscience which reacts to the political and
social projects of the day.

There is room, and need, for such a witness. From time to time
men give the impression that we must obey man rather than God.
The president of a large concern may say that they are in business,
not a philanthropic agency. Somebody must tell them that they
are not free to abandon the divine command, "Thou shalt love
thy neighbour as thyself." A leading politician may say—as one
did say—that in the government department with which he is
concerned they deal with finance and not with morals. Obviously
they are not Professors of Ethics; but it is none the less a grave
statement. How can a country deal with juvenile delinquency and
teach the messenger boy not to steal a five dollar bill, if high
officials have no concern with morals?

What then is the duty of the Christian fellowship? The day is
long past when every time the government takes snuff the church
has to sneeze; when every social trend has to be accepted because
it is the will of the people, even in defiance of the living God.
Spread through all the country are the commoners of the Christian community, one in Christ and in His service. By his words
and deeds let each fellow of the fellowship live the redeemed life,
in private and in public. There is a witness to be given on the

town council, in the teaching profession, in journalism. If Christians have penetrated the trade unions they have the opportunity of showing their associates that man does not live by bread alone—or by cake either. Those whose business is salesmanship, who serve at counters or call from door to door, and spend their hours amid the turmoil of an ephemeral world, can show the light that is eternal when they encounter their fellow men. The business executive can be a father to his employés; employés in turn can make it easier for a hard employer to see the grace that is in Christ.

Let the Christian fellowship awake and let every commoner in its membership serve God with all his heart. He should be encouraged by the sure prospect before him. Strongholds will be thrown down; the kingdoms of this world will become the Kingdom of our God and of His Christ; and He shall reign for ever and ever. Then He Who is King of kings and Lord of lords, the only Ruler of princes and presidents, the Sovereign Lord of parliaments and congresses, of tyrannies and democracies and anarchies, then He in the matchless splendour of His grace will be all in all.

THE BRIDE OF CHRIST

IT HAS BECOME the custom in recent years to speak much of the church as the body of Christ. It is a sound New Testament phrase. It fits in well with the illustration of the one body and its many members. They differ in function and in degree of weakness or strength, of honour or dishonour. Yet they constitute the one body. Throughout the whole there flows one life, and the Head is Christ.

Now the fact must be faced that this is a metaphor, used as an illustration of doctrinal truth. It cannot be literally true, for instance, that some part of the church is an eye and some other part an ear. It may be quite correct to say that some part "sees" more clearly as it looks away to Jesus or that another part "listens" more attentively to the Word of God. But how far can this process go? Are we seriously going to argue that some parts can "smell" heresy? What duty should we assign to the stomach or liver?

This is not literal truth but it is still truth. And it must be seen in the whole context of the New Testament teaching about the church. There are other metaphors. When our Lord said that He was the Vine and His disciples the branches He was pointing ultimately to the church. It is as believing men abide in Him that they enjoy life, eternal life. We must not go very far beyond that. Could anyone, in the interests of literality, assert that the "branches" are made of wood? There are undoubtedly "wooden" Christians but we must not prove it from this passage. Our Lord is the Good Shepherd and we are the sheep of His pasture. That does not mean that some Christians are "woolly." We are God's temple, God's building and God's husbandry—His cultivated field. All these and other such metaphors are an apt expression for some Christian truth. Danger arises if one illustration is pressed too far.

This has happened in regard to the church as the body of Christ. Christ is the Head of the church: He is its Lord; He commands it and guides it. And if the body is joined to the Head, then the body enjoys life communicated to it by the Head. But it is not the same metaphysical life; it is soteriological life. The church is not "alive" by sharing in the life which the Second Person of the Holy Trinity shares with God the Father. Christian "life" means that a believer is no longer under wrath; is justified by faith; and is in fellowship with God through Christ and will for ever be in such fellowship.

The metaphor must not be taken beyond its New Testament meaning. If we do so take it we run the risk of grievous error. It is possible to emphasize the church as the body of Christ in such a manner that the result is idolatry. It is very much open to doubt, for example, if the church is the extension of the incarnation. It seems to lead to a sort of ecclesiastical pantheism. If there is any extension of the incarnation it is to be found in the Holy Spirit. The body of Christ is composed of sinful men, partially sanctified no doubt, but with sin still remaining in them and not completely eradicated. As Luther taught, sin is like a man's beard. A man may have a shave today, but it will not last for ever. As long as he lives he needs another shave tomorrow. It cannot possibly be right, therefore, to regard the church as a "part" of Christ.

It is true that we are told that when men speak like this they are not thinking of the empirical church. But what other church is there? For all eternity the people of God will be praising Him for His goodness and mercy. They will never deify themselves while they cry "worthy is the Lamb that was slain." If the church is "part" of Christ then presumably the ungodly died for themselves. Yet men still speak as if the Godhead consisted of God the Father, God the Son and God the Holy Church.

It is sometimes asserted that "the body of Christ" is the richest conception of the church to be found in the New Testament. We grant the value of making the distinction between, say, the branches of the Vine or the sheep of the flock, and the body. But is the "body" the richest conception? We suggest that the figure of speech, the metaphor, of "the bride of Christ" is richer still. It contains the truth involved in "body" and at the same time retains the distinction between Christ and His people. Christ loved the church and gave Himself up for it. It is not natural to speak of a head loving its own body in this way.

The "body" suggests the unity between head and body. So does the metaphor of marriage. "He who loves his own wife loves himself." He has abandoned his father and mother and has become joined to his wife and the two have become one flesh. Here is the unity. But the apostle still says that husbands ought to love their wives as their own bodies. That "as" is important. Husband and wife are one; they are "one flesh." But the husband must still love his wife. We may speak sentimentally about "two hearts beating as one" and we know what is meant. But they do not beat as one. That would be a freak of nature. Husband and wife, though one, are distinct from each other. Each has a separate consciousness and each feels a separate pleasure or pain. The one may sympathize with the other; but if I break my leg or cut my arm deeply, it is I who feel the consequent pain, not she. Husbands and wives may, and do, disagree. And one of them dies before the other. Count the many widows and widowers in the world and see if husband and wife are distinct!

So the church is the bride of Christ. The people of God are one with Him but eternally distinct from Him. He is never separated from them ("Lo I am with you always. . . .") but He is always distinct from them. He is the Saviour; they are the saved. He died for them; by the mercy of God they did not die for their sins and never will. He knew the bitterness and woe of being separated from God ("My God, my God, why hast Thou forsaken Me?"), that they might be bound to Him for ever. He is the eternal Son of God; they are children by adoption and will live for ever; but their existence does not stretch backwards into a past eternity. He is Son of God by nature; they are children of their heavenly Father by grace.

The biblical metaphor of marriage is used in both Old and New Testament. God is the Husband of Israel; the church is the bride of Christ. This is ultimately the key to explain the reference to God as the "jealous" God. Not everybody understands this term and many dislike it. But it has nothing to do with the petty jealousy of suburbia or of keeping up with the Joneses. It does not imply anything like sulky irritation. It is perfectly appropriate in the context of marriage. For look at marriage as we see it today. Some marriages fail simply through an absence of "jealousy". A famous advocate, with long experience of the lawcourts to guide him, once said that the wife who says that she is going to live her own life and go her own way and have her own men friends is just a plain—fool. But the husband who tolerates it is hardly possessed of much more wisdom. He ought to be "jealous." This does not mean that he is perpetually criticizing his wife for speaking politely to men. There are the doctor, the minister, the school-master, the taxi driver, the streetcar driver, the grocer and dozens of others whom she can hardly fail to meet. No, jealousy does not mean a surly restriction on social grace. It means that a husband can say that this woman is my wife and not yours. She lives with me and not with you. She depends on me and not on you. She married me and not you.

Marriage is exclusive. It is one of the few instances where we can use the word "my" without the constant fear of selfishness. The husband or the wife has the right, in law, in morals and in the Christian faith to say "my" husband, "my" wife.

When God is said to be "jealous" it means that He has the exclusive right. These people are Mine! It is a right exercised in righteousness and love, but it is a right none the less. So Christ as the Bridegroom is entitled to the constant faith, love and service of His people. He is their Creator and Redeemer, has won their allegiance and has guided and kept them by His providence, and has promised to keep them for all eternity.

In the best sense of the word His attitude is "possessive." He asserts His position for He is Lord. He claims His own because He has purchased the bride with His own blood. It is best for the bride to remain faithful to Him and it is in her own interests to do so, to say nothing of the love she ought to have towards Him. But ultimately "the Redeemer is thy Husband."

This is not the possessiveness which is egotistic, boring and irritating because it is at heart suspicious. It is the possessiveness of a love which never fails and of a wisdom which is never wrong and of a knowledge which sees the future as clearly as the present. It is the duty and the delight of the church to be the object of the Saviour's love.

Marriage may begin with a relative ignorance. Engaged couples think they know each other but in the first year of marriage they learn that there are depths of mind and character perhaps never before suspected. Illness and anxiety draw them closer together, and in crises they discover undreamt powers of sympathy and endurance. In marriage husband and wife come to know each other almost without limit, and such knowledge allied to love leads to utter confidence.

So it is with Christ and His church. He knows His people and with the passing years of discipleship they learn Christ more and more. In a sense no man really knows Christ: no man knows the Son save the Father. But this is the unlimited knowledge which is required to reach down into the depths of the mind and heart of the Son of God. In another sense His saints do know Him. Serving Him in faith and love for half a century a believing man learns the ways of God and finds times without number that it is best to trust even when he cannot see. Later experience and reflection shows that the Lord knew best. Thus he comes to know His Lord and the Lord always knows Him.

Such intimacy in mutual acquaintance is known in prayer. Dinsdale T. Young once asked: "Who talked with God as Spurgeon did?" Husband and wife can discuss anything and everything on the basis of their mutual love, knowledge and confidence and the same is true of God and His authentic people. Matters of immediate or remote concern; problems large and small; temptations and dangers which would be unmentioned in other company; matters domestic, financial, business, social or spiritual; everything can be spread before the Lord for His approval or dissuasion, His guidance and His help.

It is one of the glories of the Christian faith that in it we find our freedom. "If the Son shall make you free ye shall be free indeed." In our obedience to Him we find our peace and our freedom. It might be thought that our very personality is lost in obedience but in fact it is made. We are never so personal as when we obey the living God. We surrender, and instead of being absorbed and lost in God we are found and made in Christ—and in God. In marriage we surrender—and find, not lose, our individuality.

The minister who spends time in pastoral visitation will discover among his "shut-ins" a man incapacitated for long years, spending the prime of life in bed. He is not rich, for his disability pension is but modest. But a loving wife tends and cares for him through the long months and years. Toil has left its mark. She is no longer the radiant bride of two decades ago. Her hair is flecked with grey and there are lines on her face. She is cook and housekeeper, gardener and nurse—and she never thinks of sending in a bill. All is done for love. And her stricken husband never sends for the police or other instrument of the law to enforce her service. Why should he? She has no need to be conscripted but serves with loving heart—and hands. In true marriage, service may need some inspiration to restore a flagging spirit but compulsion never. Love gives its all, without reward, without bargaining, without conditions. So Christ gave His all on the cross without waiting for men to agree to terms; and so should the church serve Him in a faith which operates through love.

So the church is the bride of Christ. It is a rich metaphor, as we have seen, but its meaning has not yet been exhausted. Every

bride has a history, both before and after marriage, and the same
is true of the church. In fact the word "bride" describes in brief
compass the story of the whole church and of each individual
who is an authentic member. (We are not here including "nomi-
nal" Christians.)

To begin with we should notice what may be called an original
apartness. We hear of child marriages in India and of marriage
ceremonies in which bridegroom and bride are young children of
tender years. Even if this practice were adopted or approved, the
fact remains that people are not born married. It may be that in
some families there is an expectation or a hope that two babies
will eventually marry. The fact remains, however, that they have
to be married. They are not born in the married state.

This is true of the Christian and of the church at large. There
are certainly people who when questioned will say that they were
born Christians, and we know what they are trying to say. They
were born in a Christian home, where God's Name is known and
reverenced. They were brought up to believe in Christ as Saviour
and Lord. I once had a student who could not remember a time
when he did not love Christ—to use his own words. All this is a
cause for thankfulness. But the language is unfortunate, "born a
Christian." The point is that even those who have "always"
known and loved Christ have had to be introduced to Him; they
had to be taught; had to be shown how to pray. They were not
born believing. If they had been moved to another home, an
unbelieving home, at six weeks of age, it is unlikely that they
would have been brought up as Christians. They might never
have come to faith.

The "original apartness" implied by the marriage metaphor is
taught in the scriptures in other language, so that we are not
unduly straining a metaphor to breaking-point. The prodigal son
of Luke 15 went into a far country: he is apart from his father.
And the apartness is not merely physical and geographical. It is a
spiritual attitude. As soon as he could get away he did—with the
cash!

The gentiles were at one time apart from Christ: alienated and
foreign. And the Jew, privileged though he was, could become a
gentile in the sight of God. He had the law and the seal of circumcision; but if he transgressed the law his circumcision became
uncircumcision. He was reduced to the position of a gentile. A
way is open, however, in the gospel. In Christ Jesus those who
were once far off have been made nigh by the blood of Christ.
Far off and near: it describes an original apartness, abolished on

God's side by the cross and on man's when he exercises faith in Jesus.

In this situation of mutual separation we see next an astounding love. We see in the history of a marriage a man who loves a woman, often at a distance, before introductions have been made and even when he may not even know her name. He loves her.

This is applicable to the church which is the bride of Christ and to its members. God so loved the world. Christ loved the church. He loved me—as St. Paul exultantly tells the Galatians. God's love in Christ is not only logically prior to our response; it is chronologically prior. Before we loved Him, before we answered in faith, before we even knew Him or of Him, He loved us; and some He loved who have never responded. This is a bridegroom's love.

With such a love it is not surprising that there follows a search to win the bride. And it is a downward search. The bride in this case is not a radiant beauty who by her beauty and character virtually causes the bridegroom to fall in love, even against his better judgment. She is unattractive, repellent, ugly in feature and character, and has no wish to be won. But the bridegroom of set purpose gave her his love. She did not make him or inspire him. It was an act of His will.

The great scripture passage to prove this is the *locus classicus* on the incarnation in Philippians 2. At every point the Bridegroom went lower, all for the purpose of finding and making her His bride. From the heights of heaven itself He emptied Himself by taking the form of a slave and assuming a likeness to men—He was like them in everything except sin. Now on earth in human style He went lower still: He humbled Himself by His obedience to His Father and did not cease until He had reached death itself. Even here He went lower still, for it was not any death. It was not the death which could be claimed by a gentleman. It was a criminal's death, death of a cross. And it was all for one purpose. In the language of soteriology He came to save sinners; within the present metaphor He searched, ever further from His celestial home and ever lower on the human scene, for the bride. She was not yet His bride. But He did everything necessary to enable Him to find her and lay His hand on her and claim her as His.

For He made a costly purchase. He did not come bringing *things* which He had in abundance. He might have transferred the wealth of heaven to earth, to sweep the bride off her feet, just as a man of wealth might attract a simple village girl with his glittering possessions. But this would have cost Him nothing. He

has an infinite number of possessions and can create more whenever He so wills. And it would have left the bride untouched.
Riches can attract for the moment but they cannot satisfy. Even
if the bride constantly enjoyed the wealth, she would have
"married for money" and there would have been no real love or
fellowship. He would not have delivered her from mental and
spiritual bondage. Instead He took another way. "Ye were bought
with a price"—redeemed with the blood of the Lamb. The bride
is free to come. But will she?

So far she knows nothing of His plans. But now He makes a
gracious proposal. He sends His messenger to acquaint her of His
loving purpose and He comes Himself as well with a loving
invitation on His lips. "Come unto Me. . . ." is the word which He
has sent on in advance, and He repeats it Himself when He
encounters her. Femininity is wont to shrink at times from high
adventure through a lack of suitable apparel. The existing wardrobe contains nothing but old clothes, all ready to be discarded.
But He provides them too. "He hath clothed me with the garments of salvation, he hath covered me with the robe of
righteousness . . . as a bride adorneth herself with her jewels."
The doctrine of justification by faith can be asserted—and
preached—in the terms of a marriage metaphor.

When the proposal is accepted the Bridegroom has always a
spirit of possessiveness. The bride is His for ever. This is symbolized doctrinally by baptism, which is "indelible." It is not
repeated. "To be baptized into the Name of the Lord Jesus"
means to pass into the ownership of the Lord Jesus. Many of us
have knowledge of family arrangements whereby a newly bought
house is put "into the name of my son." It means that the son has
the ownership of the property. Or an employer may pay some
money into a bank to be put "into the name" of one of his staff.
While the money is in the employer's hand it is his. When it is
put "into the name" of his employé it has a new owner. The
employé now owns it.

We must not think that in the marriage metaphor the bride, as
being owned, is a slave or a chattel. Our Lord treats personality
as personality. "I have called you friends." The bride, however,
is His and He always claims her as His. This is the meaning of an
expression which we used to hear frequently, the Lord's *peculiar*
people. It does not mean that they are odd. It means that they are
His own.

Paul was stating the same truth when he said that he bore the
brand-marks of Jesus in his body. It is not the figure of marriage

but the theological truth is the same. Looking at the scars which disfigured him, as a result of his missionary labours and his persecutions, he sees in them not merely a record of stripes received and dangers passed. They are the brands, perhaps even the tattoo marks, which identify the owner. The bride belongs to the Bridegroom. The church belongs to Christ. I am His.

So begins the intimate fellowship between Bridegroom and bride, between church and Head, between believer and Saviour. Just as in marriage the tie persists but husband and wife have to take thought and care to "make the marriage work"; just as they remain married and yet have to avoid being "unhusbandly" or "unwifely"; so it is with Christ. The church is in His hands and no man will pluck the church out of His hands. Yet He told us to "abide in Him." It is clearly something which we must do, or He would not have so commanded us. The thoughts of the bride must not stray towards "other men." The thoughts of believers must never be deflected from their own Lord. There is but one Saviour.

And the Bridegroom protects the bride. The church is one with Christ and He is one with the church. Nobody ever hated his own flesh. He rather provides it with food and cherishes it. So Christ does to the church. Bridegroom and bride are "one flesh" (though ever distinct), for we are members of His body, and He does not neglect His own "flesh." The church on earth may suffer but she is always under His loving care and protection, will survive on earth as a corporate institution and live in heaven with Him in exultant worship and praise for ever and ever.

We can now drop the metaphor and state the doctrine. The church is one with Christ but eternally distinct from Him. It is never separated from Him but is never to be identified with Him. It has been chosen by Him not because of itself but in spite of itself. It has been redeemed by Christ and won by Christ, and its future is bound up with Christ. It belongs exclusively to Him. In the Christian experience of its members—and apart from its members there is no church; the Bridegroom has no bride—we see one side of the mutual knowledge and mutual love of Christ and His people. They surrender their will and find their character and joy.

When we come to think of it, the church as the bride of Christ is an aspect of "the word of the cross." It maintains the high ideal of "knowing nothing except Jesus Christ and Him crucified." For the church is "the bride, the wife of the Lamb."

II

THE MEANS OF GRACE

I ONCE READ AN exciting adventure story which at the time gave
great pleasure. In the course of the narrative the three leading
characters were trapped. The villain of the piece had them at
his mercy. He had locked them in a room from which there was
no escape. Door and window were barred; the chimney was
blocked up; and even the glass was boarded up, high above their
heads. There was no way out—and from a secret source carbon
dioxide was being pumped into the room.

This was the end.

But one of the prisoners found that the keyhole of the massive
door had not been taken into account by their captor. It had not
been blocked up. Putting his mouth to the hole he sucked in the
life-giving air from outside. The second and the third man
followed him in turn. And for a long time the strange, stooping
procession went round and round in front of the door: suck—
move aside—breathe out; suck—move aside—breathe out; suck
—move aside—breathe out.

So it went on. When in due course the villain came and un-
locked the door to inspect his (as he thought) unconscious vic-
tims, he was met with a concentrated onslaught which was as
violent as it was unexpected. Our heroes had survived to fight
another day.

Such is the inventiveness of the writer of the "thriller." It is a
magnificent illustration for us to use as we think of "the means of
grace." For believing men live in the world and according to our
Lord's teaching it is a very dangerous place indeed for His
disciples. The deeds of the world are evil. It does not know the
Father. It hates Jesus, it hates His disciples and it hates the Father
also. Hence arises the persecution of Christians. Within the limits
of our illustration we can say that we are trapped in the world.
We cannot go and live elsewhere. And "carbon dioxide" is being
poured in for our spiritual ruin.

But we have a keyhole. Our Lord is the Way and the Truth and the *Life*, and through the keyhole we are able to draw in the life-giving air. The breath of life is accessible.

But what is the "keyhole"? It is important for us to realize what is meant by the expression "the means of grace." Take the term "means" first of all. It signifies *that through which* something comes—here "grace." We can think of a channel, a canal or a culvert. We can think of a great pipe-line *through* which gasoline is sent from the well or the refinery to the consumer, perhaps hundreds of miles away. In Canada we may remember the pipe-line which conveys "natural gas" (not gasoline) to users who live far from its source. In the present instance we are thinking of a keyhole *through* which something comes.

We have spoken of grace and have suggested that it comes to us *through* something. We must now observe that "the means of grace" is a convenient and quick expression which has to be carefully expounded. For there is no such *thing* as grace. It is not a substance or an entity. How could it be measured? Could we speak of half a pound of grace; or of ten miles of it? It is an abstract term. Grace does not exist apart from a gracious personality.

If anyone is in doubt, let him consider a similar term, love. Love does not exist in itself. It is not a thing, a substance or an entity. There are only people who love. The same is true of anger or any other abstract term. Anger is not found apart from angry persons or animals.

Grace, then, is to be found only in a gracious person. For us this can only mean Jesus. He is the embodiment of God's grace. In Him we see God being gracious: in Him God in the highest loves men in the depths. In Him God freely gives what men do not deserve and cannot earn. In Him God justifies the unjustifiable and pardons the unpardonable. In Him God stoops low and loves the lowest. Grace is love looking downwards, coming downwards. It is "surprising" love: it is under no obligation and yet it loves; it feels no attraction and yet it loves. God in Christ loves sinful men.

Grace, then, is to be found only in a Person, Jesus Christ our Lord. And the traditional phrase, "the means of grace," describes the ways in which our gracious Lord is accessible to His people. He meets His disciples in response to their movement towards Him. He is graciously present when they turn to Him and seek His help. But when and where do they turn to Him?

There is a strong body of opinion in the Christian community which would think first and foremost of the Lord's Supper. "Here,

H

O my Lord, I see Thee face to face." This is the first line of a Protestant hymn and it must be given a Protestant, not a Roman, interpretation. It is a fact that Christians do meet their Lord in the Communion Service and they find Him gracious. He is not limited to the bread and wine. In the whole service the gospel is set forth and the believing man meets Him. We shall say more of this later. For the moment we observe that, in the terms of our illustration, the service is a "keyhole" through which the vital air comes to us; and that the Lord's Supper is a final check on the pulpit. If the Word is denied or distorted by the preacher, it is affirmed in the Communion. "As often as ye eat this bread, and drink this cup, ye do show the Lord's death till He come."

But how often can we draw in breath through this keyhole? The practice of Christians varies. For some it is once a quarter; for others once a month. Some attend the Communion Service once a week; and some every day. The last represents a maximum. By tradition Christians do not attend the Lord's Supper more than once in a single day.

Suppose that a Christian does attend every day. Can he live on that? Whatever the answer may be, there is no need for him to try. There are other services of worship—morning and evening give us two keyholes, so to speak—and in the preached Word there are keyholes without number.

The preaching of the Word is a means of grace. The living Christ is present. The Word uttered, the promise given, is matched by the Lord Who is offered to the people for their reception. Does the preacher offer pardon and peace in the Name of the Lord? The same Lord is present to give pardon and peace to the man who believes. Does he offer strength to the burdened; comfort to the wounded; joy to the sorrowing? The living Lord Himself there and then strengthens, comforts and encourages, provided men put their trust in Him.

We should note carefully that it is not the services in themselves which are a means of grace. It is conceivable, though perhaps unlikely, that the services might be "conducted" in a secular spirit. The services are "used" by the living Christ and in them He draws near to those who draw near to Him—in faith. If faith is absent, the blessing will not be received. The gracious Lord is present but His gifts are refused.

So one great keyhole, one means of grace, comes under the head of public worship. But it can be reasonably asserted that we cannot be in church all day and every day. This is very true. Even if there were non-stop services we should have to allow for the weakness of the flesh. "The spirit is willing but the flesh is weak." God knows this as well as we do and in His mercy has given us other keyholes, other means of grace.

There is private reading of God's Word written. One of the remarkable features of recent years has been the number of books published which deal with the scriptures. There seems to be a spirit of inquiry; a desire to know more about the Bible and its contents. All this is to the good, as far as it goes. But the Bible is not only a subject for academic study. It is the spiritual food for the soul. We must avoid at all costs the unhappy situation of the man who is the academic master of the scriptures and no more than a novice in Christian experience. The Bible is to be read and studied believingly and prayerfully. When the heart of man is open to the Holy Spirit, then the scriptures are opened up to him for travel. For the Bible is like a vast territory of virgin soil: no railways, no roads, no system of communications. But led by the Spirit a believer can find his way through them and discover rich food. And as he comes across truth written he finds that Truth living is speaking to him in grace. Christ communicates to him through the book and Himself corresponds to the book.

Does he read of the Good Shepherd? The Good Shepherd is present with him. Does he read of a Christian duty? The living Lord presses his task upon him and promises him His aid. Does he read of One Who binds up the wounds of the broken-hearted? He shows the Lord his wounds and claims His promise.

This is a keyhole of which we might make more use than we do. Most of us have far more opportunities than we take up. Even so, at times we cannot approach this keyhole. We cannot read the Bible in our office, when we ought to be, in honesty, about our employer's interests. If we are students, we cannot read the Bible in the middle of an important football match. If we are teachers, we should not read the Bible when we are supposed to be teaching chemistry or mathematics. Is there no keyhole for us when we are working under authority, under orders; when we must concentrate on tasks set us by those set over us?

As a matter of fact we are surrounded by keyholes day and night. We see this in the story of Nehemiah, the cupbearer of Artaxerxes. He was in attendance on the king, and became afraid when the king pointedly asked for an explanation of his sad expression. Nehemiah told him of the waste which was once Jerusalem. "For what dost thou make request?" asked Artaxerxes. Was this an opportunity or a trap? Did it call for swift thought or for instant flight? Before answering, Nehemiah had immediate recourse to his keyhole. "So I prayed to the God of heaven."

Prayer is always possible. It need not be a long utterance. The heartfelt cry of faith carries more weight with God than a polished literary utterance from a cold heart. Our chief danger as Christians is not that we shall deny the efficacy of prayer. We believe in it; but do we practise it? When reminded and moved to pray we often agree with ourselves that the idea is good—but not yet: there is not time or opportunity. Our problem is not the philosophy of prayer; it is the practical problem of getting started.

In such circumstances it is a good plan not to dismiss the thought of prayer but to reason briefly with ourselves. Let us admit that we cannot pray at the present moment; let us face the fact that the time is inopportune; let us agree with ourselves that we must postpone prayer. And then let us *pray one sentence*. Let us decide before we start that it is to be only one sentence. We cannot object to the loss of time then.

This method has certain advantages. It avoids a series of postponements which can lead to a prayerless week. A single sentence will keep us in touch with our Lord, if we pray thus whenever the thought strikes us. And we shall have made a start. And we shall often find that having begun we shall go on. The hardest part of prayer is the beginning. The most difficult sentence is the first. Plan to pray one sentence at once; and others will follow. If they do not, for any reason like that of the duty of work or even of conversation, the line will have been kept open. In other words, when you are too busy to pray, face the fact and do not be beaten by it. Pray one sentence. Either it will lead to more; or it will keep you in touch. Use the keyhole!

Public worship; private Bible study; private prayer: these are the means through which the believing man learns more of his gracious Saviour and encounters Him. There is in addition the less "formal" factor of social intercourse with fellow Christians. This may be on the large scale of a public meeting; or it may consist of no more than conversation with a few Christians—even with one. "They that feared the Lord spake often one to another." Without necessarily setting out to do so, one may encourage the other with what he says or in the manner of his saying it. From such apparently casual talk may come new vision, new resolve, new hope. And it is not a secular "pulling of ourselves together." It is a reinvigoration of faith in the living Christ, a new pledge of discipleship, a new expectation of guidance and blessing. The Lord Himself is not absent from such social talk.

It is significant that when Paul prayed that his readers might grasp what is the breadth and length and height and depth of it, and might know (blessed paradox!), the love of Christ that passes knowledge, he was careful to include the phrase "with all the saints." For however deeply a man knows and loves Christ, he cannot know Him fully if he remains isolated. Human life is so broad and the experience of Christ so rich that it takes the whole company of the redeemed to know His love. There are young and strong Christians who have never known what it is to be bereaved. Those whose sorrow has been turned into joy by the Lord can tell them of His faithfulness and goodness in their distress. Weak Christians can catch the contagion of a lively faith and learn of the Lord the Strengthener. Christians harried by affairs of business or civic life can see the effect in human life of the peace of God. And those who have not yet entered fully into their inheritance in Christ have placed before their wondering eyes the experience of full salvation, of full assurance, of "boldness."

This is ultimately the principle of John Wesley's "class meeting." The sharing of Christian experience enriches the whole group with new knowledge of the Lord's dealings with His people, and fans into lustier flame the love which men bear to Him. But it is not restricted to a "meeting." The ordinary conversation of godly men can do the same.

Paul knew the value of sound speech, not only in the preacher but in the rank and file. Just as a builder should not, and generally does not, use beams of wood which have rotted; so in common talk we should not use "rotten" words. They are not good for the purpose of building, of edifying. Let the layman (as well as the preacher) use words as solid in their way as the builder's beams and planks. Thus he will give grace to his hearers.

Grace can be given by a layman. He does not have to be a lay preacher or a lay reader, authorized to perform some tasks usually regarded as the responsibility of the ministry. The grace of God is not restricted to the sacraments or the ministry. It may come in the friendly talk of a Christian man. "While they were talking . . . Jesus Himself drew near."

Having, we hope, made the point clear, we must now speak of the two sacraments or ordinances as some prefer to call them. In our quite correct New Testament emphasis on preaching we must not neglect the other commands of our Lord. We begin with the service which is repeated at regular intervals in the life of the church. What exactly is the Lord's Supper or Holy Communion?

It is first of all an act of obedience. Our Lord said: "Do this in remembrance of me," and we do it. Most pastors at some time in their ministry have to deal with people of whose Christian faith they are certain but who are strangely reluctant to come to the Lord's Table. "I don't see the need of it." This may possibly be true. They may be suffering from a blind spot. But it is ultimately a failure of faith. Our Lord did not say: "Do this when you see the need of it." It is an absolute command. How often has a leader—sometimes a politician or high officer of state—told his followers: "You must trust me; I cannot give you more information." How often has a soldier gone blindly into battle in obedience to orders, though in his heart he may fear that "someone has blundered." But Christ has not blundered; and He has given us "more information," as we shall see. He has told us to do it, and we ought to do it.

The Lord's Supper is secondly a mode of remembrance. We may be told, and are told, that we can remember Him in other ways. This may be quite true, and we ought so to remember Him. "Remember Jesus Christ risen from the dead." But there are different ways of remembering a person, on the ordinary human scene. A man may be remembered for his benefactions: he gave the town a football field. Some will remember him for his political life: he "cleared up" the town. A poor woman may remember him because he forgave her a debt when her children were hungry. A minister might remember him for his reciprocal kindness. On a dark day in the minister's life he came to him and said: "You stood by me when my wife died. Now I've come to stand by you now that your wife has died."

Similarly our Lord might have chosen to be remembered in one or other of many different ways. He might have asked His people annually to gather round some products of the carpenter's art, for He was a carpenter. He might have initiated some memorial service the centre of which was medicine bottles— empty. He was the great physician but He did not need the doctor's tools. He might have required an annual memorial sermon. These suggestions are unlikely if not grotesque. In fact He chose to be remembered *theologically*.

This should be pondered. We are urged, quite rightly, that in the preaching of the gospel we must make the message "understanded of the people." As far as possible we must speak in their language, and use illustrations which are simple to grasp and which shed light on the subject. But ultimately the gospel cannot be preached apart from a theology. One might think that "Christ died for our sins" is simple enough. But it is ultimately a theological statement. Who is Christ? What is sin? What was the effect of His death? If we say that the answers to these questions are to be found in the scriptures, we are correct. But they are still theological. Could anything be more theological than the Epistle to the Romans?

Our Lord commanded the use of bread and wine but He did not set up a rite of silent symbolism. If He had done so, its meaning would eventually have been lost. The bread and wine, as things, symbolize what is unfolded in words. Thus the mode of remembrance is twofold. It employs things, bread and wine, and we are not at liberty to change them. We should have no right, for example, to use meat and coffee. And it employs words, words of theological import. "This is My blood of the covenant shed for many *for the remission of sins*."

Christ Jesus came into the world, as we have seen, for the purpose of saving sinners. He has chosen to be remembered for the act which made salvation possible. His shed blood is linked with the remission of sins. The service of remembrance is therefore a reminder to the Christian of the essential gospel—and he needs the reminder. "Tell me the story often, for I forget so soon." And it is always a corrective for the preacher. If a man distorts or denies the very gospel which he was ordained to preach, the communion service corrects him without comment.

Thirdly, the Lord's Supper is a focus of participation. As St. Paul tells us, the cup is a participation in the blood of Christ; the bread is a participation in the body of Christ. The term "body" means—Jesus. "Blood" means this same Jesus, sacrificed on the cross for us. The two together, body and blood, mean Christ crucified, and in the service we share in Him Who delivered Himself up for us.

But believing men have already received Him. As many as received Him, to them He gave authority to become children of God, even to those who believe in His Name. Christ Himself put the same truth in another way. If a man loves Him, he will keep His Word; and His Father will love him; and Father and Son together will come to him and will make Their abode with him.

Such an experience has to be kept alive. This is difficult to express, because we must not give the impression that God in Christ is received by men, and then departs and has to be received all over again. This would suggest that a man is repeatedly regenerated or converted. Christ dwells in the heart of the believer but the experience of receiving Him, of knowing that He is there, has to be constantly refreshed. In a famous passage we learn that

Christ stands at the door and knocks. If a man hear His voice and open the door, He will come in to him and sup with him. The church of Laodicea was "lukewarm" but it was a church in the New Testament. Are we forbidden to see any believers in it? If a member receives Christ for the first time, it is conversion and regeneration; but if he be a lukewarm Christian, he renews his experience when he opens the door. Similarly Paul could pray that the Ephesian Christians would so exercise their faith, that Christ would take up permanent residence in their hearts. He has already called them "saints" and "faithful in Christ Jesus." Christ was therefore already in their hearts. He prays for a renewal of the experience.

Now in the communion service believing men come together as men in whom Christ dwells. They come, not to receive Christ for the first time, but *to renew the experience* of receiving Him and knowing Him. They may have been converted at different times and in different places. Now, together and as one, they come seeking each to receive the one Christ; to share in Him. On the same occasion, in the same meeting or service, they each seek afresh the same Christ, with the refreshment of spirit which they originally experienced when first they received Christ.

They do not necessarily go over the details of their own conversion. This might become no more than introspection. By dwelling on Christ crucified, and reminded of that great sacrifice by the bread and wine, and in a spirit of receptiveness, they repeat and renew their attitude of faith which they had when first Christ came into their heart. Christ is already in their hearts, for they are believers. But as they ponder His deep love for them shown in the cross, in their experience it is as if He were coming into their hearts for the first time. *Unitedly* they share in Christ. The service is then a focus of participation.

The Lord's Supper is fourthly a profession of unity. Paul sees in the one loaf a deep symbolism of the oneness of the Christian community. We all partake of it, a fact which shows that we are one body. The bread is shared out but Christ is shared. Each member present receives part of the bread; but each believer has Christ in His fullness—not a "part" of Him. It follows that each member is like every other member. Each is a sinner; each has been redeemed by the blood of Christ; each has put his trust in Him; each has received Him into his heart. All are thus in the same position, in Christ. But all are members of the one body. They belong to Christ the Head. Therefore they belong to one another.

Certain logical—and practical—deductions can be drawn from this. Christians cannot logically come to the Communion Service and then quarrel with one another. They may honestly disagree about certain matters but it must only be in love. By taking part in the service they have openly admitted that they are disciples of Christ, that they belong to His body and that they belong to one another. To be consistent they must maintain this profession when the service is over. It is a particular case of "Forgive us our trespasses as we forgive those who trespass against us."

These implications are not realized as they should be. Public men especially should be on their guard. What are we to think when a prominent churchman makes a bitter attack on another churchman? Or when politicians of opposing parties engage in an exchange of malicious hostilities in the newspapers or on a public platform? It may be that in a democracy policies are hammered out in controversy; but when communicants take part what should be dominant in their minds—the claims of the party or even of the state, or the commands of God? The membership of some politicians is an embarrassment to the church.

Again, Christians cannot attend the Communion Service and then repudiate one another, ignore one another or engage in that loveless action which "cuts him dead." There is a story told of the young Spurgeon who after a service of communion ardently spoke to a gentleman much older than himself. The response was stiff and frigid. "I do not know you." "I think you do," said Spurgeon. "We have both been in our Father's house and we have sat round the table together." The gentleman saw the point—and apologized.

This must not be misunderstood. We are not advocating a jolly *camaraderie* which despises all social grace and politeness and fails to give respect to age. Its real spirit is "in Christ," which involves humility rather than a backslapping forwardness.

Fifthly, the Lord's Supper is a mutual pledge. "This cup is the new covenant in My blood." This is the "better covenant" of which the writer to the Hebrews speaks. For there was an older one which lacked the "better promises." Through Christ crucified God says to His believing people: "I will be their God and they shall be My people." Reminded by the wine of the blood of Christ shed for them, they learn afresh that God is their covenant God and that they are His covenant people. The tokens of their redemption, the bread and the wine, tell them that God is loyal to His people. As His covenant people they belong to Him and their participation is an act of loyalty to Him—and a promise. As God has pledged His loyalty to them, so they pledge their loyalty to Him. Thus pledges are exchanged between God and His people.

It would be for the benefit of our soul's health if we reflected more on this truth. We leave the service, pledged men. We have re-affirmed our membership of the covenant. We have said, in effect, that "I belong to Christ." This should be a stimulus to us to live the Christian life as well as profess it: a life of faithfulness and obedience.

On the other hand, wavering Christians are not unknown. They wonder if God has really accepted them; wonder if He really will keep them in the pilgrimage of life; are anxious about what will happen on the Day of Judgment. Their attitude might not unfairly be summed up in the cry: "Lord, I believe; help Thou my unbelief." In the Communion Service God deals with their condition. The bread and wine tell them with loving repetition that God has received them. Is there any more convincing testimony than the blood of Christ? And if God has not spared His own Son—*for them*—and with Him freely gives them everything; is He likely to let them go now? The love that shines in the cross is the love which is active in providence. God keeps His people—and in the Communion Service He tells them so. And He keeps them to the end—and beyond. By faith they have been justified. All their sins that ever were or will be have been washed away by the shed blood of Christ. The eschatological justification has anticipated the Judgment Day itself. For them it is no longer an open question whether "they will go to heaven or not." "They will see His Face." God in Christ has pledged Himself to His people. In the Lord's Supper He repeats His pledge, re-affirms it and illustrates it. The bread and wine measure His immeasurable love and loyalty. And those who receive these His tokens by their very reception pledge their loyalty to Him.

Finally the Lord's Supper is a service of preaching. We do not here mean that there is a sermon preached from the pulpit by a preacher. There may be; but even if no sermon is given "ye do show the Lord's death till He come." The service in itself tells the story of the cross. It is a matter for the deepest regret that in some churches the Lord's Supper is the only evangelical element. The pulpit is strangely silent about the cross and its New Testament meaning. But while the pulpit is silent the Table is eloquent, telling to the eye as well as to the ear the gospel of our redemption. Christ died for us.

We may criticize the church for its irrelevance and the services for their dullness. We may charge the preacher with being ineffective or unorthodox. But as long as the Lord's Supper is celebrated there is a witness to the gospel and Christ is preached. This should not lull the preacher to sleep but should spur him to the proclamation of Christ. One life-time is not long enough to explore and open up the unsearchable wealth of Christ! But if the preacher fails the Table tells the gospel story. This is a further reason why believers should not neglect the Lord's Supper.

This raises the whole question of whether the communion is "necessary to salvation." I remember as a small boy being perplexed and troubled about this. I attended church with my parents regularly and sometimes was present with them at a Communion Service. When the time came for the congregation to receive the bread and the wine ("the administration") my parents went forward with the other people to the communion rail while I stayed sitting in the pew. I was almost terrified at all this "going up to the front in the presence of all those people"—self-conscious boy that I was.

At the midday meal one Sunday I asked my father a question. "If a man were a believer but never went to the Communion Service, would he go to heaven?" There was a long silence. My father was a wise and saintly man. But I doubt if he realized how important the question was to me. In a sense my eternity hung in the balance! I could not see myself "going up to the front." Finally he said something like this: "If he really trusted Christ as Saviour he would go to heaven; but he would go as a disobedient Christian."

This brings us back to where we started. Christians ought in obedience to our Lord to "do this in remembrance of Me." And with all the blessings which follow obedience we may well continue to use the time-honoured expression, "the means of grace."

The same applies to baptism. It is commanded by our Lord and He should be obeyed. In the New Testament it is in a missionary setting. The church is continuing its outward thrust and converts are baptized, for it is the duty not only of the convert to be baptized but of the church to baptize him. Whatever view a Christian holds today about infant baptism—and its sharpest critics, strangely enough, are not Baptist scholars—in the New Testament it is a rite administered to believing men. This is the norm or standard and it is followed by all the churches on what used to be called "the mission field." Sometimes such a field is remarkably near to home. An Anglican clergyman in North America introduced me to two Moslems and told me with shining eyes that he was going to baptize them the following Sunday. This is the

New Testament pattern and any baptism of infants must be interpreted in the light of the baptism of believers and not *vice versa*.

Baptism is the focus or concentration of a man's faith to a single point. All of faith that has gone before: all the high points of his spiritual experience in which he has felt very close to Christ; all the depths in which he has had to fight for his faith in the absence of the spiritual glow; all the hours and days when his faith has been neither on the mountain top nor in the valley but in the plain, a pedestrian, plodding faith rather than a soaring or a crawling faith: all is gathered up into a kind of spiritual "instantaneous moment" of obedient expression of his faith: "I believe in God through Jesus Christ our Lord." He sets the seal on all his subjective believing. Before witnesses as he is, he brings his inner (not necessarily secret) faith out into the open as he obediently submits.

Other metaphors might be employed if we so desired. He has burned his boats. He has crossed his Rubicon. Any "blur" in his faith has been corrected and given precision, for the service is one of words, a sort of document to which he has signed his name and set his seal. And on the other side, all that he has learnt hitherto of God's grace; all his experience of having been received by God in Christ; all is sealed by the living God. God here and now accepts him.

Neither must be separated from the other. In baptism the believing man and the accepting God meet. That is to say, baptism must not be considered in the abstract, as a power or force which has a spiritual effect apart from the God Who accepts and the candidate who believes.

In some states the law requires that a man who signs a legal document like a deed transferring stock or shares to a purchaser must, at the time of signature, put his hand to the paper and say "I deliver this as my hand and deed." Little seals are stuck to the document, just beside his name which he has just written. They are made of stiff paper, red in colour, circular, and have gum on the back to make them stick to the deed. For ordinary people, as opposed to those who have an official seal, they constitute a seal.

Now the shares may have been bought and sold on the Stock Exchange and the transfer deed has to be registered with the company which originally issued the shares. It sometimes happens —or happened—that an examining officer found that a deed had no seals stuck to it. He might have returned it to the lawyers or stockbrokers who sent it in for registration, asking for the defect to be remedied. He instead takes a little box of red seals, takes out as many as he needs and sticks them to the document beside the signatures. Each completes the deed and to all intents and purposes was under the man's finger when he said: "I deliver this as my hand and deed."

A little box of red seals: let us dwell on that for a moment. Seals are seals, and they authenticate a document. They say, in effect: "this man really did sign his name." But of what value is a box of seals by itself? Of what value is a seal, in isolation? It authenticates nothing, for there is nothing to authenticate.

It is like that with baptism, which we have called a seal. If God and man do not meet in baptism, what can possibly be sealed? If a man is an unbeliever he cannot seal his own faith in Christ; and God does not seal His acceptance of a man who does not put his trust in His Son. In the absence of faith there is nothing in the man to be sealed either by himself or by God.

This is a discussion or an exposition of principles. When we come down to actual occurrences we see their import—and their importance. For example, when Lord Haldane was a young man he submitted to baptism, under a natural parental pressure. As soon as the service was over he faced the congregation and told them that he did not accept their doctrines or the sacrament, which he held to be no more than an external ceremony. There and then in measured words he repudiated the church and its teaching. Could anything possibly have been sealed?

This should be pondered by all those who hold rigidly to a doctrine of baptismal regeneration. If baptism, by the mere fact of having been administered, effects regeneration without regard to the antecedent necessary conditions, then what is its value? Stalin went to a theological seminary and was presumably baptized. If he was regenerated, what is the value of regeneration? If he was not regenerated, what has gone wrong?

Given the fulfilment of the necessary conditions, namely that the accepting God meets the believing man, baptism may be described in three ways. It is, first of all, an affirmation of new ownership. (Sometimes notices are displayed outside a store to attract customers. They say that the store is now "under new management." Baptism affirms that, and more than that. It is not only a question of who "manages" a man; it is concerned with who owns him.) When a man on repentance and faith is baptized *into the Name of* the Lord Jesus Christ it indicates that he has passed into the ownership of the Lord. The candidate affirms that he no longer professes to own himself: "Jesus is Lord." And God in Christ likewise affirms in baptism that He is the Owner.

Not everyone desires to keep his own property. Some women "clear out" their wardrobe every year because they are renewing their whole outfit. Some men will discard a jalopy by driving it to the local dump and leaving it there. And when a family moves from one city to another, how much accumulated "junk" is just "thrown out"! A man I know threw out half a ton a few years ago. But God does not abandon the human rubbish which is fit for nothing but the scrapheap.

We hear much about the value of the human soul and its infinite worth. We should notice that it has value because Christ died for it. Christ did not die for it because it has value. That would come near to justification by grace and works combined. And a repentant sinner finds in baptism that he who apart from Christ is less than nothing passes into the ownership of the Lord Who accepts him and keeps him. He does not repudiate His ownership.

Secondly, baptism is an admission of new clothes. Biblical references to clothes are interesting. John the Baptist was clad in camel's hair and a leathern girdle which, combined with a diet of locusts and wild honey, seem to sum up the austerity of an Old Testament prophet. The man Legion, from whom our Lord sent the unclean spirits into the Gadarene swine, was seen after his cure "sitting, clothed and sane." His clothes qualify him to enter civilized society. The man without the wedding garment was not allowed to stay at the wedding breakfast: he obviously did not "belong" to such company. The returning prodigal was given the best robe to celebrate his welcome home: his body, emaciated by sin, must be covered.

Now St. Paul tells the Romans to "put on" the Lord Jesus Christ, just as one "puts on" a garment. He is not referring to conversion as they already believed. He seeks the renewal of that experience in which they first put their trust in Christ and His righteousness was imputed to them. Imputed righteousness is an alternative expression for justification by faith. When a man trusts Christ he is given new clothes.

> Jesus, Thy blood and righteousness
> My beauty are, my glorious dress.
> 'Mid flaming worlds, in these arrayed,
> With joy shall I lift up my head.

The apostle does not mean that they once put on the righteousness of Christ but have since discarded the new clothes and must put them on again. They are still, as it were, dressed in Him in

God's sight. But he wants them to refresh their experience. (This is similar to what we have seen in the Lord's Supper as "focus of participation.")

Between the first surrender to Christ in faith and the renewal of the experience, of which we have been just speaking, there is the experience of baptism. Paul tells the Galatians that their sonship comes through their faith, which is his battle-cry in the Galatian letter transposed to another key. Instead of speaking of justification by faith he now speaks of sonship by faith. But the reason he gives is arresting. "For all you people who were baptized into Christ, put on Christ." But they had already done this when they first believed. Baptism is thus a renewal of the experience, a focus, once more, or a concentration of that experience when the candidate first "put on" Christ.

Once more God and the believer meet. The believer admits (an alternative for "confesses") openly that he stands, not exactly "in borrowed plumes," because they have been given to him through faith, but in clothes which he did not make or buy or earn. He admits that he is clad in the righteousness of Christ. And in baptism also God admits and owns him as dressed in Christ. God looks on him, a repentant sinner, and He sees—Christ. God does not go back on this. He has accepted the believer for ever, in Christ. And if the Christian is tempted to wonder at his own sinful nakedness and to be doubtful of himself, he should remember, like Luther, that God in his baptism admitted him to Himself, dressed in Christ. "Baptizatus sum."

Thirdly, baptism is a pledge of a new life. Are Christians to remain in sin, asks Paul, in order to magnify and multiply the grace of God? Superficially, it is a tenable position. The more I sin, the more God forgives. His grace is the more manifest. But Paul counters this. We died to sin, i.e. we repudiated our sinful self and became insensitive to sin's blandishments. We were baptized into Christ's death and buried with Him, through baptism. Christ was raised from the dead. Paul does not quite say "and so were we." The purpose of baptism is *in order that* the parallel might be fulfilled. Christ was raised and we ought to walk in newness of life.

He later develops this, and speaks not in terms of newness of life but of resurrection. "You were buried with Him in baptism, in which also you were raised with Him *through faith.* . . ."

In other words, baptism tells a story and brings an experience into a focus. The Christian was not actually present at Calvary, and indeed Christ died in order that he might not die. But the pattern of death, burial, resurrection is seen in the experience of the Christian. All his self-repudiation and final ("burial") ethical self-renunciation; all his experience of spiritual power through the living Christ: all is gathered into a focus in baptism. Self dies. The candidate "crucified the flesh." And the new self is raised. There is nothing mechanical about this. It is "through faith." What has been happening in his spiritual life is brought into a focus, enacted and felt in baptism. He yields to Christ—as he has done already. Christ takes over—as He has done already: the *ego* no longer lives but "Christ lives in me." When Paul wrote like this he still had a vigorous "self": he was neither a machine nor a block of wood. But it was a self like a musical instrument, played by Christ.

In baptism, then, the believer explicitly and openly repudiates his sinful past life and pledges himself to discipleship, to obedient service of the Master and Saviour. And Christ accepts his pledge and returns it. With the channel of faith open Christ will pour into it all His power for a victorious life.

It should be noticed that in baptism, no less than in the Lord's Supper, the cross is central. There is a difference of language. In the Supper we speak of Body and Blood; in baptism we think of death, burial and resurrection. In both it is the cross of Christ.

What has been written so far represents, I believe, the New Testament teaching and practice concerning baptism. It is the norm or standard, and if infant baptism is the custom it must be governed by the New Testament. There has been much heart-searching in recent years by paedo-baptists and much self-criticism. We do not propose in this book to enter into controversy as such. But given the fact that infant baptism is to be found almost universally, we must discuss it, especially as some hold strongly to a doctrine of baptismal regeneration.

There are three interpretations which may be called the mystical, the rational and the evangelical. The mystical view holds that in baptism the baby is there and then regenerated on the spot. The view is tenaciously held by some even to the point of magic. But it is undermined by the story of Nicodemus. "The wind bloweth where it listeth . . . so is everyone that is born of the Spirit." This does not describe the newly baptized baby. Baptism, *in itself*, is not enough; conversion cannot be inherited or "caught" by infection or contagion.

The rational view has more to commend it. It holds that baptism is the rite of initiation into the visible church, making the child participate in the privileges of church membership and fellowship. He is brought into a new environment. Nothing "happens" to the baby in baptism: his name presumably goes down in black and white as someone who "belongs" to the church, though on a sort of junior basis. In time he will be "entitled" to go to Sunday School and later to join the Confirmation or Church Membership Class. He is progressively though no doubt simply able to enjoy "fellowship" with the other members of the church.

This interpretation labours under the difficulty of offering privileges ("the environment") which can be had without baptism. Clergymen in the Anglican communion, for instance, find from time to time in their Confirmation classes, especially with older people, that there are a number of baptisms to be administered before Confirmation. If this is due to recent conversion, then we must thank God for a new believer in Christ. But what of those who have been "brought up in the church"? What of those who have been through the Sunday School and have regularly attended the Sunday services of the church but for some reason have not been baptized? Their lack of baptism has not "kept them out." They have enjoyed exactly the same privileges as their baptized friends. As a matter of fact the baptized babies have not been brought into a new environment by baptism. They are brought there because their mothers carry them there and send or take them to Sunday School and to church.

The rational view thus avoids an extreme theory of baptismal regeneration but at the expense of a certain lack of realism. There are many people, unbaptized, who have close associations with the worshipping church and engage in many of its activities. It is hard to see how they can avoid being in a new environment.

The evangelical view is proleptic or anticipatory. It recognizes God's initiative in man's salvation and expresses that fact by baptizing the child before he can himself respond in faith to God's grace. We can best understand the position by means of an illustration. Let us suppose (and it is not difficult) that there is a scientist in North America with a world reputation whom other countries are eagerly seeking to attract. He thanks them for their compliments but declines their offer. Then one day a delegation with full powers comes to him from one of the universities in, say, Australia or New Zealand. They make him a princely offer. He thanks them but still declines. He is somewhat apprehensive of the consequences. It means leaving his native land and going to a far country, unknown to him. He has as yet no friends there. It is a serious matter to resign his Professorship. There is many a slip 'twixt cup and lip. What security has he?

In the end he is persuaded by an unusual argument. We have full powers, they say, and we represent the Senate. Anything we do will be implemented by the university. We have made all the preliminary arrangements with your own university. If you will consent, we will have a formal ceremony of installation here on your own campus. Invitations are already under consideration to the leading men in your own country: to Governors or Lieutenant-Governors, to heads of universities and colleges, to professors in the faculties of science, to leaders of all the churches, to judges and prominent lawyers and to everyone of significance in the community. Before all these witnesses the Chancellor of the university, who is here with us, will solemnly make use of these very words: "I hereby install you as Professor of Nuclear Physics in the University of X."

If such a ceremony were seriously contemplated and seriously carried out, the Professor would be installed while still in North America to a Chair on the other side of the world. He would be the Professor of his new university; *but he would have to go there to receive the emoluments.*

It is somewhat like this in the evangelical view of infant baptism. The baby is "installed" as it were. But he has himself to respond in faith to the invitation "Come unto Me. . . ." before he receives (not the emoluments but) the blessings. Baptism is not unconditional, and the baby is not born again until he believes.

We have not said anything about *which* babies should be baptized. Should it be all and sundry who may be brought or should it be restricted to the children of Christian parents? There is room for a thorough investigation of the "theology," or the Christian view, of the child. If, in spite of all the paedo-baptist self-criticism, infant baptism is retained in the universal church, then undoubtedly the evangelical interpretation is the best.

We must now briefly sum up. By "the means of grace" we mean that the living, gracious God is accessible to His people. He has abundant blessings for them if they will but take them. Through Christ we have access in one Spirit to the Father.

THE SECOND ADVENT

ABOUT A CENTURY AGO politicians and statesmen gathered at the London Conference. Their deliberations resulted in the plan for the unification of Canada in the famous "Confederation." There is in existence a picture of these men. Some of them are great names in Canadian history—Galt, Tupper, Cartier, Tilley, Lord Monck, and the great "Sir John A." himself. These were distinguished men. In the picture, however, it is not their distinction which impresses us but their appearance.

How old-fashioned they seem to us today! Their long coats and stiff high collars; their heavy watch-chains and their beards; to say nothing of the attendant page-boy's eton collar and coat; all are alien to us today and speak of the century from which they come. We may smile at the strangeness of a former fashion. We may be glad that no longer do many of us have to wear the massive Prince Albert watch-chain and that we have the convenience of the wrist-watch. We may be thankful that in dress as in much else we have been emancipated from the formal. All this is quite natural. But it does not make the book untrue. There stands the picture in a book of Canadian history, marking the style of an age that is gone. But the teaching of the book is not affected.

So it is with the language of the apostle Paul's Epistle to the Thessalonians, which we make our point of departure in considering the Second Advent. This well-worn term, justified by the language of Heb. 9: 28, describes the climax of history which is brought about by our Lord's return or "Parousia." The language is pictorial: use is made of eschatological imagery and some find a use of Jewish apocalyptic which is old-fashioned.

Why does Paul speak like this? It is because he is grappling to express a truth and no other kind of speech was available. The events he is trying to reduce to writing have never happened before and are unique. Inspired man that he is, he must use the best human language at his command if he is to be "understanded of the people."

He has to deal with a situation. The church of the Thessalonians is alarmed and grieved. Some of their number have died. For us today the death of a church member may not be "news" but there was a time when it was a new thing. Just as there must have been the first Christian baptism, the first Lord's Supper after Pentecost or the first ordination to the ministry, so there must have been the first Christian death. Apparently not knowing of the death of Stephen, the first Christian martyr, the Christians of Thessalonica felt the impact of the death of some of their own members as if it were an absolutely new experience for the church.

In consequence they were deeply troubled. They had listened with glowing interest to the apostle's teaching about the return of the Lord. Now some of their fellow-Christians had died. Would they miss the blessings of the Parousia? Keyed to the pitch of earnest expectation and hope, had they seen the cup dashed to the ground when it was at their very lips? Longing to see the Master face to face in all His splendour, were they to know in contrast nothing but the dullness of the grave? Were the surviving Christians to be beset with uncertainty? Is death the great anti-climax?

These questions which arose in the Thessalonian church are relevant today. Equally relevant are the apostle's answers. Does death miss the blessing? Does the river of life reach the ocean or does it end in a swamp? Does the pilgrim see a light in the distance calling him on, only to fall by the wayside in the dark? Has he been pressing on towards the heavenly kingdom, to find his end in a grave of earth?

No! says the apostle. *There is a future, and it is Christ's.* To what does everything lead? Some would speak of the philosopher's "end" or purpose and find it within the process of life itself. But there is a goal to which the whole creation moves. The One Who was present in power at the beginning is not absent at the end.

Some people speak as if the universe produced itself. Others see a design without a designer; some speak vaguely of nature and some, equally vaguely, of "God." But they speak as if they did not know this God. This is not the teaching of Holy Scripture. The passages which relate Christ to the creation imply that the Creator is known. We are not left with an unknown Creator. All things ("the totality") have been created through Christ, says St. Paul. The Epistle to the Hebrews speaks of God's Son "through Whom He made the worlds." John tells us that all things were made through the Word. The meaning is plain. It is not only that Christ is God's Agent in creation, though that is true. The

universe comes to us from the creative hand, or rather the creative word ("God said. . . ."), of One Who is known in Christ.

This God does not change. The "all things" which have been
created through Christ continue in Him, and in Him they cohere
in the system which they are. Christ "sustains" all things, keeps
them going, "operates" them. Thus the God Who created is
known—in Christ; and the God Who sustains is known, in
Christ.

But in addition the "all things" have been created "unto Him."
As we learn from the Epistle to the Hebrews, God appointed His
Son to be Heir of all things. As the creation moves forward to its
predetermined end, there at the end stands—Christ. The God
Who is Master and Lord of all, past, present and future; the God
Who created, sustains and brings His creation to its appointed
goal is no unknown God. He is the God and Father of our Lord
Jesus Christ, through Whom, in Whom and for Whom He made
all things.

This Christian truth does away with much theorizing and is a
comfort to every believing though anxious heart. We are told
that the earth is cooling, for example, and that in time to come
we shall be as cold as the moon: all value and all life gone, with
men gradually frozen to death, going out not with a bang but a
whimper. It may look like that to the scientist. But what if something happens before the temperature falls too low? There is a
future for men—for some men, believing men. The Lord of the
future is Christ, their own Lord and Redeemer.

Again, we have been warned increasingly of the danger of
atomic destruction. Let loose nuclear warfare in the world and
not only might humanity be annihilated but the very globe might
disintegrate. True, it may appear so to the political observer or
news commentator. We may have been near to it at the time of
the "Cuba crisis." But if it ever came it would not be a secular
smash and ruin and no more. Christ is in control, even of atomic
disintegration, and believing men will continue to be in Him. For
them there is a future, because the future is Christ's and they are
His.

Some men pin their faith in the so-called immortality of the
race, though the threat of atomic dissolution must weaken their
faith. This view sees the generations coming and going for ever.
Generations die and die for ever but there is always a new one to
take their place. There is small comfort here for the individual.
"Ever dwell on the future?" asked a character in a modern novel.
"Ever dwell on the future? It's a dismal period after a certain

age." Dismal indeed; unbelief is shrouded in gloom even though for an hour it enjoys "the pleasures of sin." But the Christian faith is a gospel for the aged as well as for youth. "Ever dwell on the future?" Yes, indeed; it belongs to Christ and Christ is God's—and I am Christ's.

Secularism has nothing to offer but an ultimate pessimism. It has been well expressed by Shakespeare.

> Tomorrow, and tomorrow, and tomorrow,
> Creeps in this petty pace from day to day,
> To the last syllable of recorded time:
> And all our yesterdays have lighted fools
> The way to dusty death. Out, out, brief candle!
> Life's but a walking shadow, a poor player
> That struts and frets his hour upon the stage,
> And then is heard no more: it is a tale
> Told by an idiot, full of sound and fury,
> Signifying nothing.

No speed, no greatness, no wisdom, no reality, no exhilaration, no meaning, no prospect! This is not much to die on! But for the Christian there is a living Saviour Who has redeemed us from an empty life, from an insignificant tradition and from a counterfeit apostolic succession in a very unoriginal sin. There is a future and it is Christ's. We do not continue in sorrow like the secularists who are devoid of hope. For if we believe, as we do, that Jesus died and rose, we believe in conformity with this that God will bring with Jesus those who passed through the door which they thought was marked "Death" but as they came nearer to it found that it contained the notice: "Jesus."

We have not, of course, exhausted the apostle's teaching. In the present day, however, it is something to know for sure that there is a future; still more to know that it is in the pierced hand of the Redeemer. But Paul would have us to understand that *there is a rule, and it is Christ's.* The Lord Himself will come down from heaven. . . . This is the crux of the problem to the modern mind. We no longer live in a three-deck universe, and if the world is like a sphere a presence in the northern hemisphere means an absence in the southern. Such, at any rate, is the argument. But what is the apostle trying to say?

Christ is already ruling the world. He is exalted to the Father's right hand. The Father has committed to Him the administration of the universe. All authority is given to Him in heaven and on earth. But He rules from the unseen. He is not here now in the way in which He was here in the days of His flesh. If He were, we should have to rally to Him, somewhere. But though His localized presence is not to be found He is not absent. He is here by His Spirit, "God's method of the presence of Jesus." This is not the last word on the Holy Spirit, the Third Person of the Blessed Trinity, but it is helpful in interpretation. It is through the Holy Spirit that we are able to know Christ. It may be doubted if we know the Holy Spirit in distinction from Christ. "He shall glorify Me." When we are nearest to Christ in spiritual communion and are most intimate with Him, it is due to the Holy Spirit Who effaces Himself in order that Christ may be known. The Christ Whom we know by the Holy Spirit is Lord. Present in the hearts of believing men as Saviour and Lord, He is Lord not only of those who believe in Him but of the whole universe.

A famous admiral has said that the sailor may forget the church but that the church never forgets the sailor. He finds here a worthy symbolism which points to the Unseen Hand which is at the helm of all things. He testifies that though deafened by the roar of guns and blinded by their smoke, and lurching, slithering and falling through the pools of blood, the sailor is yet conscious of that Unseen Hand.

Now at the Second Advent the unseen rule of Christ becomes the manifest rule of Christ, bringing history to its goal and climax. This is the meaning of the statement that "He will come down from heaven." It is surprising that men have found difficulty here. It is not the first time that the Lord "has come down from heaven". He came down at the Incarnation, as our Lord told Nicodemus. But it does not mean that He came down from the sky or that He travelled in space. It is said that Mr. Khrushchev sent a man into space in order to find out if God were there. If he had first consulted the church, any biblical scholar could have saved the Russian revenue millions of dollars! The Lord is not localized in space. He is in that realm which transcends space and time. The Second Advent is thus a new mode of His presence.

What other language was available to the apostle? If men thought at that time that heaven was "up there" it was the most natural thing in the world to speak of the Lord's coming down from heaven. That is why the Ascension is described in literal terms to describe a literal event. There was no other way for our Lord to show that He was returning to His Father. But the emphasis is not on the travel through space but on going to God, exalted. The "travel" is the least important aspect, though it was bound to be expressed thus.

Note the pageantry and the majesty and all the brilliant accompaniment of His royal rule. He will come "with a shout of command" as befits the manifest Ruler of all things. The archangel's voice calls for the attention of all the world and the trumpet fanfare imports a due solemnity to what has been a worldly scene.

The meaning is plain though the details may be obscure. It is idle to say that if the Lord came to North America He would not and could not be seen in Australia. In the same spirit of objection we could argue that if He came to Jerusalem He could not be seen in Rome. This criticism could have been raised in the apostle's time and it would be interesting to know his answer. He has not given it and we must not speculate. We do not know how the Lord will appear but His presence will be manifest. This should be enough for believing men.

There is a future; and it is Christ's. There is a rule and it is likewise His. His people in Him have a future too, and the life of obedient discipleship will have abundant scope. *For there is a fellowship, and it is Christ's.* His people belong to Him now, and they will remain His. God will bring with Jesus those who fell asleep through Him. They will not be forestalled by the Christians who survive to the Parousia. On the contrary the dead in Christ will be raised, and, rising, will be joined by the surviving Christians. There will be no more sleeping in Him. There will be no more waiting for Him. Dead Christians and living Christians will be more united to Him than ever; and at the same time united to one another.

The apostle has not given us a blueprint or diagrams. It may be doubted if he meant that the Christian dead "travel" with the returning Lord and on arrival are united to their resurrected bodies. Behind the doctrine of resurrection stands the whole biblical teaching about the nature of personality: it is not a soul living in a body but rather an animated body. St. Paul implies that at the Parousia the Christian dead will be with Christ in the fullness of their personalities and that "we," the Christian survivors, will join them to meet the Lord in the air.

This affords great scope for a critical and mocking unbelief. Before we dismiss the whole passage as a crude representation which no self-respecting modern mind can accept we should try to understand what the apostle really does say.

First, "to meet" does not mean "to have a chance encounter." The expression is full of purpose, a purpose which is in the minds of the Christians who go "to meet the Lord." Today we go to the station or airport with the express purpose of meeting someone there. We do not drift there unconsciously, "bump into" an acquaintance or friend and then say with surprise, "Fancy seeing you here!" Seeing that we set out with the avowed purpose of meeting them we should have been surprised if they had not appeared. It is precisely like that in the apostle's language. The Christians set out to meet their returning Lord. This usage is illustrated elsewhere in the New Testament. When Paul was nearing the imperial city the Christians in Rome heard of his circumstances and travelled to Appii Forum and Tres Tabernae to meet him. They did not stumble on him by accident. Indeed "to meet" suggests almost an official welcome for a newly-arrived dignitary. They did not wait for the apostle to reach the city itself. A deputation went out to offer their greetings and to give him a more or less formal escort.

So in the Parable of the Wise and Foolish Virgins. In the middle of the night the cry went up, "Behold, the bridegroom; come out to meet him." The wise virgins were ready.

Such is the love which Christ the Saviour inspires in His people that when He returns their previous longing for Him is turned into welcome and they "go out to meet Him." Should not disciples join the angelic escort? The language may be figurative, symbolic or call it what we will, but the spiritual truth remains.

But what are we to say about being caught up? This has suggested to impious minds the picture of the saints travelling through space, with blowing skirts and ruffled hair and all the signs of undignified embarrassment which can be imagined by the irreverent. Such an attitude magnifies difficulties and does not deal with them. We ought to ask rather what is the nature of the "force" which seizes them. Is it a force? Or is there some other possible explanation?

We may find a clue in the writings of Hippocrates, the great Greek physician of the fifth century B.C. who gave his name to many works on medicine (even when written by his disciples) and to the famous "Hippocratic oath" in which the physician undertakes to be loyal to the best medical tradition. There is a passage in one of the treatises attributed to him in which he speaks of a "stone which *snatches* the iron," the "stone" being the lodestone or magnet.

Here is a possible interpretation. The Lord Who said, "I will draw all men unto Me" continues to be the same magnetic Personality. At His return His people cannot wait, as it were, for His arrival: drawn to Him as by some mighty magnet, they go

out to meet Him. The language is picturesque but the spiritual
import is plain. Believing men will not be troubled by sneers at
travel through space. They know their Lord and learning of His
coming they are impelled towards Him, drawn like iron to a
magnet.

But is it "into the air"? It may be so. But there are more
important matters than geography! The New Testament speaks
of "the ruler of the authority of the air" and of "the spirit that is
now active in the sons of disobedience." It would seem that the
"air" has evil spirits as its tenants. If that is so their day is limited.
The place where they hold evil sway is the meeting place of the
Lord and His people. The universe is swept clean!

Such is the greeting and the meeting with which the Lord's
loyal and longing subjects acclaim Him. The importance of the
teaching may be judged by its practical value and the use Paul
makes of it. Comfort one another with these words. In this way,
that is, with this introduction, we shall ever be—with the Lord.
The non-Christian will here see nothing of value at all. The vague
and puzzled theist will not see much more. The professed
Christian in whom the fires of discipleship burn low may be
moderately interested. It is only the genuine disciple, who takes
his faith seriously and loves his Lord and Saviour, who will be
moved to gratitude and joy. Eschatology is thus the test of the
vitality and the intensity of our Christian faith. It was because the
apostle had received so much from Christ that he pressed on in
faith and service; it was because his ardent ambition, "that I may
know Him," was progressively fulfilled as he pressed on that he
looked for yet more; and it was because he looked for the climax
of history, with his Lord at its centre in command, and not for a
secular fading away of all things which would make him and his
fellow-believers of all men most to be pitied, that he rejoiced in
the prospect of being "for ever with the Lord."

When will this be? It is imminent but not necessarily immediate.
The Second Advent will be unheralded and unannounced but not
unexpected. It will be sudden but will be preceded by signs. It is
said that in 1944, when the opening of the "Second Front" was
near, every day for a month a large number of ships put out from
England as if to invade the continent of Europe. Any day might
have proved to be D-Day. When it finally came there was no
prior warning, "this is the day." It was sudden when it came and
imminent before it came. There was no warning; but the Ger-
mans must have expected it. So it will be at the Parousia. The
church has always been, and always must be, expectant of the

great day, "until He come." But it will come like a thief in the night. And this will begin that joyous eternity in which we shall be "for ever with the Lord."

And when we are with Him, what then? The New Testament uses a rich symbolism in which to express the wonder and glory of heaven. Grace will reward those who have borne the burden and heat of life's day and all pain and sorrow will be at an end. Spiritual aspirations will be realized, knowledge and understanding will deepen, and perfection of mind and character will continue in endless growth. Redeemed men will not be static. They will be "always complete but never finished." And the perfection of their character will be matched by the perfection of their environment.

All this is true but it might be interpreted as a secular heaven. It is the thought of a secularized heaven which has led some people to say that it is not "fair" for men like Hitler to be excluded. Should not forgiveness be extended to the worst? Let everybody go to heaven!

The defect of such views, apart from their unscripturalness, is that they tend to dwell exclusively on the "things" of heaven and the human beings who enjoy them, and God in Christ is omitted. But for the Christian heaven is to be "for ever with the Lord." If He is absent it is not heaven; if He is present in the fullness of His kingdom, it is heaven whether or no the environment be heavenly. In His mercy He gives to His people His own intimate presence, their own perfected character and an environment to match.

John tells us that we shall be like Him because we shall see Him as He is. How do we see Him now? We do not see Him at all for He is spirit not flesh; and though He retains His glorified Body He is not here bodily but by His Spirit.

With this proviso we may go on to speak of "seeing." We talk of "seeing" the hand of God in providence and of "seeing" the work of the Spirit. In this figurative sense we can say that though we do not see everything subordinated to Him we do see Jesus crowned with glory and honour. We shall be "for ever with the Lord"; how shall we see Him then, when we see Him as He is?

We shall see Him face to face. We now see Him through a glass, darkly, as we learn from St. Paul. He does not mean that we have not switched on the light. He is thinking of the ancient mirror, probably made of metal, which gave a somewhat distorted image. We see Him in a mirror, with some obscurity.

This can be developed. Think of the man driving an auto-

mobile, and seeing in his mirror another car overtaking him. Or
think of a boy busily engaged in the task of washing his face in the
bathroom, anxiously looking in the mirror to see if his brother is
trying to enter the room to play a prank on him from the rear.
Think, better still, of a woman looking at herself in the glass and
her husband quietly stealing up from behind. If the believing
church is the Bride of Christ, let each member think of the Lord
Whom he sees in the mirror, Who comes up from behind us and
looks over our shoulder.

This is a lovely picture; but when that final day shall have been
ushered in we shall see Him face to face. There will be no distor-
tions then, and no indirectness; we shall see Him as He is, face to
face.

The authentic believer has here an authentic joy. For it implies
that we shall see Him fully, not partially. It is natural enough that
one or other aspect of our Lord appeals to different men. Like the
wisdom of God, He is "many-splendoured," "iridescent." In
earlier years we used to be able to buy a necktie made of "shot"
silk: when approached from the left it looked red; when a man
came up from the right it seemed to be green. Like the grace of
God, He manifests Himself in many ways: as Prophet, Priest and
King. Piety varies according to the dominant constitution of a
man. It tends to be intellectual to the academic, practical to the
man of will and emotional to the warm-hearted. To each of these
the Lord is the one Lord and yet is "different." To the one He is
the Word Who satisfies the intellect; to the other He is the
Saviour Who is to be served; to the third He is the fount of joy.

So with "all sorts and conditions of men" in the church
different Christians have different emphases. Paul knew how to be
abased and how to abound, which shows his power of adaptation
and his belief that there is a Christian way in which to be poor and
a Christian way in which to be rich. For some He is the poor man's
Christ; for others He is the rich man's Saviour. Some preachers,
given half a chance, would preach to the same congregation every
Sunday on the Second Advent; others seem to find their gospel
solely in the incarnation. Both will be brought together in the
one Christ Who will be fully known.

For other sections of the community other distinctions are
made. The man beset with temptation remembers with thanksgiving that "the Word was made flesh" and that we have a
sympathetic Highpriest Who was tempted at all points as we are
yet without sin. Another who yearns for a gospel of saving power
dwells on the deity of the Son of God and worships Him with the

Name that is above every name. Some live in the Epistle to the Romans and emphasize the work of Christ on the cross for them, speaking often of repentance and faith; others ponder the Sermon on the Mount and seek to stir the church to make a bigger impact on society at large. Here a man, perhaps in his youth an unwanted child, finds in the love of Christ his enduring solace, a love from which no man or angel, beast or devil, can ever separate him. Yonder there is a thoughtful citizen who sees and ponders the sins of men and thinks frequently of the justice of Christ: of the Christ Who took the place of sinners but agreed with the Judge about the verdict.

God has yet more light to break forth from His Word. We see in part and we know in part and there is still time for us to learn more from that written Word. But after the Second Advent every different aspect of the Lord which has been seen by different men will have become part of one fully revealed whole. We shall see Him face to face, fully. Our best view at the moment is but partial. Then we shall fully know Him even as we are ourselves already known by Him.

We shall see Him then in all the brightness of His countenance. We shall not be as men walking in the gloaming or in the depths of some primeval forest, barely able to discern the figures around them. We shall not have to "put out our hand in the dark and put it into the hand of God" because there is no night there and the Lord is the light thereof. We shall no longer say that we live by faith and not by sight because, though we shall always trust Him, we shall also see Him, face to face and fully, and in the brightness of eternal day.

The Bible speaks of a man who walked with God. Jesus called men to follow Him and He told them after His resurrection that He was with them. Walking, following, being with. . . . How distant is our discipleship at times; how prone we are to wander. How often we fail to abide in Christ. How many times do we "arise and go to our Father. . . ." How many more times than the preachers realize do we need the exhortation: "Come let us to the Lord our God with contrite hearts return." At that glad day He will take us to Himself, never to be separated from Him by our distant discipleship. We shall see Him, closely.

And as we shall be with the Lord for ever, so we shall see Him face to face for ever. We shall see Him perpetually, not intermittently. While we are on our pilgrimage we have our hill-tops and our valleys; our moments of spiritual ecstasy and times of dumb loyalty; seasons of refreshing and the clash of the sword in the spiritual contest; we mount up with wings as eagles and we also plod along in the desert. We have our Sundays and our week-days, our sacred seasons and our worldly cares. We have the exuberance of spiritual health and we also know the "check-up" of Lent or of Keswick "for the deepening of the spiritual life."

But we shall not always be on pilgrimage. One day we shall arrive. When we are with the Lord for ever we shall see Him face to face—without a break.

There is a cherished expression, long used in the church, which speaks of "the means of grace." John Wesley has a famous ser-mon on the subject. The "means" or channels, by which God's grace comes to us, that is, through which God in Christ is known as gracious to men, are the Scriptures (read, studied, searched, preached and heard, pondered); prayer (private and public); and the Lord's Supper and Christian fellowship generally, the gathering together of Christian people. Through these means we see Christ—until He come. After the Second Advent we shall not need the means; the "indirect" approach will be unnecessary. We shall see Him face to face, directly.

Such is the prospect for believing men. Just as eschatology is the test of the vitality and the intensity of our faith, so the promise of seeing the Lord face to face is the test of our sincerity. Do we look for things? Or do we long for the Person of our Saviour? The "things" are given to us in Christ, for the God Who spared not His own Son gave us everything with Him. But the joy of heaven is in the "He" and not in the things. Without Him sweetness itself turns to bitterness in the mouth, all loveliness is dull and brilliance loses its lustre; even the laurels of victory are flung into the dust. But with Him we have everything and He confers value on everything; and with Him, even if everything be denied us, we have everything. For we shall see Him, fully, closely, perpetually, directly, in all the light of His Person, face to face—for ever.

BIBLICAL REFERENCES

In the previous chapters references have been given very sparingly, in order not to interrupt the flow of the writing. They are here given in a roughly consecutive order.

Chapter 1. Ps. 103: 7; Deut. 26: 8 f.; Ps. 19: 1; Ps. 33: 6; Deut. 6: 4; 1 Kings 17: 1; Rom. 5: 1; Amos 3: 2; 1 Cor. 5: 7; John 1: 1 f; Col. 1: 15; John 14: 9; Luke 16: 15; 1 Cor. 1: 18; Acts 26: 26; 1: 21 f.; Rom. 6: 9; John 20: 30; Acts 4: 12; Rom. 5: 1; 1 Pet. 1: 25; Mark 5: 26; Luke 8: 43; John 16: 14; 2 Cor. 3: 15 f.; 4: 6.

Chapter 2. John 1: 3; Col. 1: 16; 1 Cor. 8: 6; Heb. 1: 2; Col. 1: 15; Heb. 1: 3; John 1: 1 f.; Gen. 1: 3; Ps. 33: 6; 1 John 1: 1 f.; 2 Cor. 8: 9; John 10: 10; 1 John 3: 14; John 11: 25 f.; 1 John 5: 13; John 1: 4 f.; 10: 28; John 1: 12, 29; Rom. 4: 25.

Chapter 3. John 1: 14; Heb. 12: 2; Matt. 5-7; Luke 4: 29; Mark 15: 21; Luke 11: 13; Matt. 10: 29; Luke 15: 8; 13: 1-5; Matt. 13: 45; 20: 1; Luke 10: 30; 16: 20 f.; Matt. 18: 25; John 14: 9.

Chapter 4. Eph. 3: 17; Gal. 2: 15 f.; Rom. 3: 2; 9:4 f.; 1 Cor. 6: 9 f.; Acts 4: 20, 29; 8: 1, 4; 11: 19-24; Phil. 3: 7-10; John 17: 3; Gal. 4: 5 f.; Rom. 8: 15 f.; 5: 5; Eph. 3: 12; 1 John 4: 17; 2 Thess. 2: 16; Matt. 13: 52; 2 Cor. 1: 3 f.; Rev. 3: 20; Matt. 28: 19; Luke 24: 47; Acts 4: 12; 2 Cor. 5: 11; Acts 19: 8; Eph. 3: 14-17.

Chapter 5. 1 Cor. 1: 18; Rom. 5: 12; 3: 23 f.; Gen. 1: 26-9; Rom. 1: 21; Matt. 5: 46; 7: 11; Luke 6: 32 f.; 17: 26-30; Rom. 1: 21 f.; 1 Cor. 2: 14; 1: 18; 2 Cor. 4: 4; Gen. 8: 22; 17: 15-22; 21: 1-8; Heb. 11: 11 f.; Gen. 15: 6; Rom. 4: 3; Gal. 3: 6; Rom. 1: 25 f., 28 f.; Luke 16: 15; Ps. 15: 1-3; 106: 3; Jer. 22: 13 f.; 1 Pet. 3: 12; 1:18 f.; 2: 21 f.; Deut. 31: 16 f.; Mark 15: 34; Rom. 3: 24 f.; Eph. 5: 2; Heb. 9: 14; 2 Tim. 2: 19; 2 Cor. 5: 21; Rom. 4: 5 f.; Gal. 4: 7; Phil. 2: 12 f.; Luke 17: 10; 1 Cor. 1: 18; 2: 2; Rom. 8: 32; Heb. 9: 22; Rom. 6: 9; 1 Cor. 1: 23; Rom. 8: 1; Rev. 5: 5 f.; Acts 15: 14.

Chapter 6. Phil. 1: 16; 1 Pet. 3: 15; Col. 3: 3; Rom. 6: 9 f.; Luke 24: 21; Rom. 1: 4; John 1: 3; 1 Pet. 3: 18; Luke 1: 21; Eph. 5: 2; Rom. 4: 25; 1 Cor. 15: 19 f., 43; Rom. 8: 11; Rom. 8: 10; Col. 1: 18; Rom. 6: 4; Col. 3: 1; 2: 12; Gal. 5: 6; 1 John 3: 20; 1 John 2: 1 f.; 1: 9; Rom. 8: 1; Eph. 3: 17; 2 Tim. 1: 10; 1 Cor. 15: 55 f.; John 1: 29.

Chapter 7. John 14: 6, 9, 26; 15: 26; 16: 7-15; Rom. 8: 9-11;
Gal. 4: 6; Eph. 2: 18; Rom. 9: 18; John 7: 43; 9: 16; 10: 19;
Mark 4: 16 f.; John 6: 67; Acts 2: 47; 1 Cor. 2: 10.

Chapter 8. John 14: 9; 1 Tim. 1: 15 f.; Acts 26 :13 f.; 9: 18;
John 3: 8; Eph. 3: 10; Rom. 3: 27; Phil. 3: 4-6; Rom. 7: 18-25;
Acts 17: 30; 1 Pet. 3: 1; 4: 17; Acts 9: 5; Eph. 2: 1-5; Rom.
6: 23; Heb. 12: 2; 2: 9; Acts 9: 7, 19-23; 26: 24; 17:18, 32;
9: 23-5; Gal. 1: 23 f.

Chapter 9. Acts 8: 39; Titus 1: 4; Jude 3; Luke 5: 10; Acts 2: 46 f.;
John 15: 1-5; 10: 11; Heb. 13: 1; 1 Pet. 2: 17; 5: 9; 1 Cor. 1: 9;
2 Cor. 13: 13 f.; 1 Cor. 10: 16; 2 Cor. 8: 4; Phil. 1: 5; 3: 10;
1 Cor. 12: 4 f.; Rom. 12: 6 f.; 2 Pet. 1: 4; Phil. 4: 15; Rom.
12: 4 f.; 1 Cor. 12: 12 f.; 3: 6 f.; Heb. 2: 14; 1 Cor. 10: 16 f.;
1 John 2: 19; Heb. 12: 22 f.; Col. 3: 3; 2 Cor. 4: 3; Acts
1: 8; 17: 23; 2 Cor. 4: 18; Phil. 2: 5; Heb. 1: 4.

Chapter 10. 1 Cor. 12: 12-27; John 15: 1-5; 10: 11; Eph. 2: 21 f.;
1 Cor. 3: 9-17; Rev. 5: 12; Eph. 5: 25-33; Rev. 19: 7 f.; 21: 9;
Matt. 28: 20; Mark 15: 34; Hosea 1: 2; 2: 16, 19 f.; 9: 1;
Jer. 31: 32; Exodus 20: 5; Isa. 54: 5; Matt. 11: 27; John 8: 36;
Eph. 2: 11-13; Rom. 2: 25; John 3: 16; Gal. 2: 20; 1 Cor.
6: 20; 7: 23; 1 Pet. 1: 19; Matt. 11: 28; Isa. 61: 10; John
15: 14 f.; Gal. 6: 17; John 10: 28; 15: 4; 1 Cor. 1: 18; 2: 2;
Rev. 21: 9.

Chapter 11. John 7: 7; 17: 25; 15: 18 f.; 14: 6; 1 Cor. 11: 26;
Mark 14: 38; Nehemiah 2: 1-4; Malachi 3: 16; Eph. 3: 18 f.;
4: 29; Luke 24: 15; 1 Cor. 11: 24 f.; 2 Tim. 2: 8; Matt. 26: 28;
1 Tim. 1: 15; 1 Cor. 10: 16; John 1: 12; 14: 23; Rev. 3: 20;
Eph. 3: 17; 1 Cor. 10: 17; Matt. 6: 12; Luke 11: 4; Heb.
7: 22; 8: 6, 10; Rom. 8: 32; Rev. 22: 4; 1 Cor. 11: 26; Eph.
3: 8; Mark 1: 6; 5: 15; Matt. 22: 11 f.; Luke 15: 22; Rom.
13: 14; Gal. 3: 27; Rom. 6: 1 f.; Col. 2: 12; 3: 1; Gal. 5: 24;
2: 20; John 3: 8; Eph. 2: 18.

Chapter 12. 1 Thess. 4: 13; Col. 1: 16 f.; 1 Cor. 8: 6; Heb. 1: 2;
John 1: 3; Heb. 11: 25; 1 Pet. 1: 18; 1 Thess. 4: 14, 16;
Acts 2: 33; Heb. 1: 13; Eph. 1: 20 f.; Matt. 28: 18; John
16: 14; 1 Thess. 4: 16-18; Acts 28: 15; Matt. 25: 6; John 12: 32;
Eph. 2: 2; Phil. 3: 10, 12; 1 Cor. 15: 19; 11: 26; 1 Thess. 5: 2;
1 John 3: 2; Heb. 2: 8 f; 1 Cor. 13: 12; John 1: 14; Heb. 4: 15;
Rom. 8: 38 f.; 1 Cor. 13: 12; Gen. 5: 22, 24.